ASSEMBLY POINT

by
Grahame Knox and David Lawrence

Scripture Union
130 City Road, London EC1V 2NJ

First published 1990 by Scripture Union,
130 City Road, London EC1V 2NJ.
British Library Cataloguing in Publication Data
Knox, Grahame
Assembly point.
1. Great Britain. Secondary schools. Morning Assembly.
Themes
I. Title   II. Lawrence, David
377.1

ISBN 0–86201–671–1

Phototypeset by Input Typesetting Ltd, London SW19
Printed and bound in Great Britain by
Ebenezer Baylis & Son Ltd., Worcester.

Acknowledgements

The authors would like to thank several staff members of Scripture Union
and Youth for Christ for their help in providing some of the ideas, assembly
outlines and practical guidance:
Chris Chesterton, Charlotte Dodds, Anita Fielder, Sue Figueiredo, Mark
Hatto, Andy Hough, Gerard Kelly, Geoff Lawton, Mark Maybury, Alison
Thurlow, Becky Totterdell, Eddie Williamson.
Their contributions have sometimes been altered, adapted or even turned
inside out to produce *Assembly Point* but we could not have done it without
their help!
Many of the ideas in the book cannot be traced to their original author
but the following items are original to the authors listed below and are
used with their permission:
The Ballad of Jesse and Jake (page 47); Colossal Consumer Christmas (page
74); God is Dog spelt backwards (page 75); Behold I stand (page 75); Gimme
Gimme, Gimme Temptation (page 94); The Trouble with Reality (page 95);
Unique (page 95): all by Gerard Kelly.
The sketch in 'The root of bitterness' (page 49); The Sausage Sketch (page
88): both by Eddie Williamson.
Mary's Visitor (page 71); A modern parable of the Good Samaritan (page
90): both by Anita Fielder.
The drawing on page 83 is by Taffy Davies.

CONTENTS

Introduction

Part One:
How to prepare and lead a school assembly

Setting the scene 11
Approaching the school 13
Involving Christians in the school 15
Dos and don'ts in assemblies 16
Using poems, stories and dramatic readings 17
Using drama 19
Using audio-visual aids 21
Putting it all together 23

Part Two:
Ready-made assembly outlines

Truth and ultimate values

1 Raise the *Kon Tiki?* 30
2 It doesn't matter what you believe! 32
3 Heads, you win! 34
4 Six years and fifty miles later. . . 36
5 Missing the point 38
6 Putting belief into action 40
7 The parable of the blower 41

Encouraging a sense of self worth

8 Losers? 44
9 The price is right! 45
10 The Ballad of Jesse and Jake 47
11 The root of bitterness 49

What Christians believe

12 The hope bulb 52
13 The God Food Guide 54
14 100 million messages every second 56
15 The slime dip 58
16 The mystery of the *Mary Celeste* 60
17 Our Father! ? 61
18 7X: The secret ingredient 67

Christmas. . .
19 A gift at Christmas   70
20 Mary's visitor   71
21 Poodles and mushrooms   73
22 Christmas is coming!   74

Easter. . .
23 Truth – stranger than fiction!   78
24 Would you believe it?   79
25 The cost of love   81

Part Three:
Additional resource material

What's the point?   87
The sausage sketch   88
Made for. . .   89
A modern parable of the Good Samaritan   90
A sense of urgency   91
Socrates and the travellers   92
Are you sure?   93
The *Impossiball* assembly   94
Gimme, gimme, gimme temptation!   94
The trouble with reality   95
Unique   95

INTRODUCTION

The need

The 1988 *Education Reform Act*, with its requirement for a daily act of 'broadly Christian' worship for every pupil, has presented a real challenge to every county school in Britain. Many teachers feel unable to lead 'Christian' worship, perhaps because they do not themselves share Christian beliefs or perhaps because they simply do not have the time to prepare adequately. In some schools Christian teachers and pupils top the list of those asked to lead worship in school assembly; in other areas leaders or members of local churches are being welcomed into schools to participate in this part of the school day. New opportunities are therefore opening up for Christians to offer help to schools, as representatives of local churches. This book is designed to equip you, the Christian visitor to the school, with the practical knowledge and skills you will need to take up the challenge of leading school worship, and to do so effectively and in a way acceptable to the school.

Subject matter

It is assumed that, as a visitor to the school, you will be invited in because you represent the Christian faith or a local Christian church. It is our experience that, on this basis, the teacher in charge will expect you to be fairly open in your explanation of the Christian faith and of what it means to be a Christian. The outlines we give in this book therefore concentrate on explaining key aspects of Christian belief as they relate to our everyday lives. Because the subject matter is deliberately limited in this way, if you are invited to take a series of assemblies rather than simply the 'one-off', you will need to broaden the scope and subject matter which you tackle. For additional ideas here, see the resources section at the back of the book and the hints in the introductory section on how to compile your own assembly.

The contents of this book

The first part of the book contains a number of short but practical articles on how to prepare and lead a worship 'slot' within an assembly. Don't be tempted to avoid this section. If you are working with others to take school assemblies there may be added value in working through these preparatory pages together.

The assembly outlines given in Part Two use a variety of themes to explain something about the Christian faith. All of these have been tried and tested in secondary schools. Lively, stimulating and imaginative ways are suggested for presenting the material. In every assembly outline you will find:

An introduction
This explains the aim of the assembly and what you will need to do in the way of preparation before the event.

Content
This explains how to introduce the assembly, and outlines the main part of the assembly input. As you use the material in this section you should aim to 'personalise' it by adding your own anecdotes, the names of local places and personalities and any relevant, current happenings in the news or in popular 'soaps' such as *Neighbours* and *EastEnders*. Prepare well enough beforehand so that you do not have to use the book in assembly; a story told is much more gripping than a story read.

Application and response
The Act specifies that 'worship' should happen in schools on a formal basis. We believe that, in a context where probably the majority of the pupils are unlikely to be practising Christians, it is fair to interpret 'worship' in terms of 'response'. The 'Application and response' section in the assembly outline draws out the point of the content and suggests appropriate responses to what has been heard in the assembly.

The type of response appropriate can vary enormously. It could be simply an increased awareness or understanding of an aspect of Christian truth, perhaps as a result of learning from the experience of others. It could be a sense of awe and wonder, evoked by what has been shared from the platform. It could be a change in attitude, such as the development of respect for something previously dismissed without thought. It could be a moment's reflection on the meaning and purpose of life. Or it could be the desire to take some practical action in response to a challenge to do so, such as organising an event to raise money for charity, or writing to the local council to ask for a bottle bank to be set up locally.

It may sometimes be appropriate to include the response of prayer. A prayer of thanks or praise could be read out for the pupils to listen to and, if they wish, make their own. This will, of course, depend on the sort of material that has been presented and on the usual practice of the school. Make a point of asking the head teacher or whoever takes responsibility for assemblies, whether it would be acceptable to include a prayer. If you do decide to include a prayer, it is important to introduce it with a phrase that allows the young people to opt out of saying it. For instance, 'I am going to say/read a short prayer now. As I do, think about the words. You might like to close your eyes to help you concentrate on what is said. If you agree with what the prayer says and want to make it your own, say "Amen" at the end, which simply means "I agree." '

An alternative to saying or reading a prayer is simply to leave a few seconds of silence after you have presented your material. Suggest that pupils use it to think over what they have heard, perhaps thinking about one point they found particularly helpful or interesting – or may have disagreed with – or to pray quietly in their minds.

Age banding

At the top of each assembly outline you will find either 'L', 'L/U' or 'U'. These represent 'lower school', 'lower or upper school' and 'upper school', indicating the age groups to which the material is felt to be most suited:

L   = 11–13s
L/U = 11–16s
U   = 14–16s

Treat these as guidelines rather than hard and fast limits; as you become more familiar with a particular school group you will become more aware of what is 'going over their heads' and what is hitting them 'spot on'. In addition, feel free to adapt the material to make it more appropriate for an age group other than that suggested.

Not all of the material in this book will suit every assembly leader or be appropriate for use in every school. Be selective, choosing outlines and methods of presentation that you know will be acceptable to the school into which you are going (or you won't be invited back!). Adapt and develop the ideas given in this book in order to make them more 'you'. To help you further along the road to creating your own assemblies, Part Three contains additional resource material.

Our hope is that this book will encourage you to take many thought-provoking assemblies, will inspire you to create many more of your own, and will help build bridges of trust between your local schools and the churches which you represent.

Part One

HOW TO PREPARE
AND LEAD A
SCHOOL ASSEMBLY

SETTING THE SCENE

Assemblies and the school day

Assemblies are a real challenge. It is no joke to stand in front of 500 restless adolescents, trying to keep their attention for ten or fifteen minutes! It is difficult to be stimulating and amusing for even two minutes when 500 faces simply stare back at you implacably.

There is much value, though, in being involved in school assemblies. A good one can set the school day off really well and stimulate the young people to think seriously about the deeper issues of life, those that transcend exams and even school itself. Your assembly could be a little gem set in the middle of a busy, maybe hassled day that will give people something to think about, discuss, laugh with and be encouraged by.

You may be sandwiched between the notices and the head telling everyone off for riotous behaviour in the corridors but, if you have prayed it through, the Lord can protect your ten-minute slot and make it a valuable time. An issue opened up in an assembly could be developed and discussed in an RE lesson or a Christian Union meeting.

Assemblies and the 1988 Education Reform Act

Many heads and teachers are turning to local churches and Christian agencies to help and resource them as they implement the worship provisions of the 1988 Education Reform Act. The Act requires that all pupils must be involved in a 'collective act of worship' every school day, which is 'wholly or mainly of a broadly Christian character.' Some explanations might be helpful here:

Assembly and worship

Under the 1988 Act 'assembly' and 'worship' are differentiated. An assembly is the time when the whole school or parts of the school, such as year groups, are gathered together for notices and other administrative purposes and perhaps to foster the school's ethos. All staff and pupils are legally obliged to be present. The act of worship is distinct from this and both staff and pupils have the right to opt out of it. Assemblies do not have to take place every day, but every pupil is supposed to be involved in a school act of worship every day, unless withdrawn by his or her parents or guardians. Generally, the two activities of assembly and worship are put together into a single 'slot'. In this book we assume you will be invited into such a situation and so refer to that entire slot as 'assembly'. The time you are allocated within it may also vary from school to school but will rarely be more than ten minutes.

Collective worship

Collective worship should be distinguished from corporate worship. By using the term 'collective', the Act acknowledges that although staff and pupils have gathered together to participate in or to observe an act of Christian worship, they do not necessarily share the Christian faith. At the same time, the Act seems to assume that a group of people from different faiths or of no faith at all can participate in an activity which accurately reflects Christian worship. Not all Christians share this view.

In contrast to collective worship, the worship of a committed body of Christians, in church for example, would be described as 'corporate'.

'... wholly or mainly of a broadly Christian character'

Beliefs and practices presented in school worship are of a 'broadly Christian' character if they are accepted across a broad spectrum of mainstream Christian denominations. It would not be acceptable to speak of practices unique to a particular denomination as though they were the practice of all Christians.

The material included in an act of worship need not be drawn 'wholly' from Christian sources. Indeed, it can be far more effective to explain a Christian truth by using sources from writers, artists, politicians etc who would claim to have no religious beliefs at all.

Practical implications of the Act

It is important to realise that the school is not providing us with an opportunity to evangelise, that is, to call people to a personal commitment to Christ. It is hardly fair to preach to a captive audience and doing so will only alienate both young people and staff. Instead of building bridges we will be putting up solid barriers.

There is no reason, however, why we should not present the Christian gospel in an assembly. As Christians we do not need to apologise for our faith. We do, however, need to be sensitive in our presentation. For example, because the majority of participants in school worship are unlikely to share a commitment to Christianity, we should not ask them to say or do things that assume their commitment.

We must also avoid presenting Christian truth in such a way that pupils are 'cornered'. That is, if they don't make the 'right' response – the one you ask for – the only other option you leave open for them is to accept that they are 'wrong'. If we present Christian truth to them we must ensure that the response we ask them for is *not* that of either accepting or rejecting the gospel.

We should avoid any hint of 'indoctrination' in what we say or the way we say it. Try to avoid making dogmatic statements or giving the impression that you are telling the pupils what to believe. Instead, share from your own experience, using phrases like, 'I believe that . . .' or 'Christians believe that . . .' In this way we can still challenge the assumptions of our hearers and stimulate them to think.

Beware!
Christians in school!

Church and school are two parts of the same community and it is good if each understands and values the other. There are probably two hurdles which you will have to overcome, however, if you are to build positive links with the school.

Firstly, young people are very cautious about 'religious' people, expecting them to be old, 'square' and Bible-bashing. Many honestly think that Christians are a particular 'type' who like praying, singing hymns and listening to long sermons. They assume that if you don't like that kind of thing you wouldn't want to be a Christian. An assembly gives us the opportunity to be seen as 'normal' people with as much personality and individuality as anyone else. Your assembly can give young people a positive picture of those who have faith in God and a positive picture of God himself.

Secondly, the staff may well be afraid that you will try to convert both them and the pupils. They are acutely aware of the 'compulsory' nature of school worship and so may deeply resent the event being used evangelistically. However, many also find the idea of taking an assembly themselves very intimidating, and will admire you for offering to do it! A well-thought-out assembly can allay their fears of proselytism.

If you gain the trust of the staff by the way in which you conduct assembly, you may find that doors open for you into other aspects of school life. It may be appropriate to offer your services in RE lessons and to the school Christian group as well as in assemblies. There is plenty of scope for contributions to school life from visitors and many ways in which parents and church members can be involved in supporting their local schools. If you are an accredited or ordained Christian minister you may be able to offer help as a member of the school's pastoral or counselling team. The help of parents is often welcomed on school trips and 'out of hours' activities.

APPROACHING THE SCHOOL

1 Pray.
2 Be clear about what you can aim to achieve in an assembly. It

should never be used as an opportunity for overt evangelism nor simply to promote a local youth event or evangelistic service, but to stimulate young people to think about the Christian faith. However, if you do wish to publicise an event or activity, following your assembly, you *must* get permission from the head first. Don't just 'spring' it on the school in the assembly.

3 Decide on who should be your initial point of contact – a Christian teacher, the head or the teacher responsible for assemblies. If possible, make your offer to a school where you already have links with staff or pupils. A knowledge of the school will help you to make the right approach.

4 Be prepared to accept a 'healthy suspicion' on the part of the school; a responsible school will not let just anybody in to take assembly! Be ready to explain the theme you will be following and to outline the material you will be using.

5 Offer to take assembly at a time when it will be of most help to the school: Christmas, Easter or Harvest, for example; *not* the first week of term or during exams.

6 Find out:
- when assembly begins and ends and how much time will be allocated to you;
- what else will happen during the total assembly time, eg notices, sports results, 'tellings off' for bad behaviour;
- what the normal pattern for assembly is and whether the school is happy to deviate from it. For instance, is there always/sometimes/never a hymn or prayer?
- the age range of the pupils in the assembly and whether they comprise the whole school or simply a part of it.
- whether pupils from other faiths will be present in the assembly and whether they will stay in for your talk. If so, which faiths do they represent and in what proportions? Is there anything you should know about relationships between the faith groups in the school?

These questions will enable you to prepare your material most effectively and, in the eyes of the staff, will help confirm your credibility.

7 If you are encouraged to choose a hymn, find out what is well known and arrange in advance with staff for a pianist and hymn books to be available. Check the words of the hymn carefully to be sure that you are not 'pushing' pupils into singing words that they may simply not believe.

8 Confirm your visit by letter. After the assembly send a thank-you letter to the head and any other teachers involved.

9 Take your diary. A good, thought-provoking assembly will lead to further invitations to the school. A series of assemblies will often create more impact in the long term than a 'one-off'. Think long term – see your visit as one of many through the years.

10 Are there other areas of school life where an offer of help would be welcomed? If your church is known to be a positive supporter of the school in every aspect of its life, anything you do in assemblies will have a much greater impact.

INVOLVING CHRISTIANS IN THE SCHOOL

One ten-minute assembly can soon be swallowed up into the school day and forgotten. But in many schools in the land God has placed Christians to be his co-workers. They may be pupils, teachers, administrators or caretakers. Through their friendships, teaching and attitudes they are providing the basic awareness of Christian belief and practice on which your assembly can build. Once you have left the school hall it will be their continuing dedicated Christian living that will enable your assembly message to take root in people's minds.

At the same time, your assembly will have a big impact on the credibility of Christians already in the school. Sensitively handled, it will be an encouragement to them and will increase their credibility with pupils and staff alike. On the other hand, you can do an enormous amount of damage to their ongoing witness in the school if you present an assembly that is aggressively evangelistic, otherwise insensitive, or simply badly organised and presented.

Remember that you are being invited onto their 'home ground' and that whatever you do will affect their own impact in the school. So it is important, as well as polite, to make contact with them as you plan your visit and to invite them to participate in the planning and presentation as much as they wish to.

Here are some pointers towards discovering and working alongside other Christians in the school.

1 When the initial contact with the school is being made find out whether there are any Christian staff at the school and whether there is a Christian Union or any other Christian group functioning within the school.

2 If you draw a blank here, use your knowledge of local churches to try to locate Christian members of staff at the school.

3 If possible, meet with some of them to pray about the assembly and to discuss what sort of topic and approach they think would be most useful. Get as much inside knowledge as possible. What sort of thing normally happens in the assembly slot that you are going to take? What is the general response from young people and staff in the school to Christianity?

4 As you plan the assembly try to do so with the Christians in the school and perhaps involve them in some aspects of the assembly presentation. Some may be able to be involved 'up front' with you, perhaps in performing a sketch or displaying visual aids. Others may have the confidence only to be porters and packers-up before and after the assembly.

5 On the big day aim to pray with the Christians in school before the assembly and, above all, encourage them. However you are feeling, try not to communicate nervousness to them!

6 Try to build into the assembly ideas and thought-starters that can be taken up by Christians in the school later in the day in their conversations with friends. Alternatively, take an approach which could be followed up with a subsequent meeting in school, perhaps hosted by the Christian Union.

DOS AND DON'TS IN ASSEMBLIES

Don'ts:

1 Don't try to make more than one clear point in the time allotted. It can be tempting for a Christian visitor to try to get across an overview of the whole of the Bible and explain the meaning of the cross all in one assembly, just in case it's the only opportunity you get to speak! This is not a good idea! In ten minutes you can only communicate *one* idea clearly and effectively, although perhaps illustrating it in several ways. It is better that people remember one thing that can be built on later than that they hear a mass of information, nothing of which they understand or remember.

2 Don't turn up late. Arriving late piles on the stress for staff as, at the last minute, they rush to try to organise something else for the assembly. Aim to arrive at least twenty minutes before the assembly is due to begin. If it is your first visit, chatting to staff will help break down any barriers of uncertainty they may have about you.

3 Don't go over time. The effect of what you've said will be completely lost if the bell goes before you've finished. You will also lose the goodwill of the staff as they see their teaching day start late and with a chaotic rush to get to the first lesson.

4 Avoid making humorous comments about staff or school meals. This can easily backfire by causing offence.

5 Don't try to explain everything! Jesus rarely explained his parables. The Holy Spirit will use what has been presented in the hearts and minds of the young people.

6 Don't make comments about other faiths or unbelievers.

Dos:

1 If you are not introduced to the school by the teacher in charge, do

explain clearly, at the beginning of the assembly, who you are.

2 Do assume little or no previous knowledge of the Christian faith. Start from where the pupils are and move them on from the familiar into the unfamiliar.

3 Do avoid Christian cliches and jargon. Explain clearly what any unfamiliar words mean.

4 Do dress smartly.

5 Do be polite and courteous with all staff. The way you respond to them is an important part of your witness.

6 Do make contact with Christians you know in the school beforehand (see pages 15–16) and let them know about the planned assembly visit. Their comments and possible involvement will be helpful.

7 Do prepare thoroughly. Know your material well and avoid using a script (except in poems and dramatic readings). Take time to rehearse sketches to get words and timing right.

8 Do involve pupils in the presentation of the assembly. Many of the outlines in this book suggest that you do this; seeing their friends up on stage is part of what makes assembly memorable for the rest of the school! However, you need to exercise care. Where the outlines suggest that you invite pupils to take part you can do so by one of these means:

- If you are confident that you can handle the unexpected, simply ask for volunteers on the spot.
- In advance, ask a teacher to give you the names of pupils who they think would be happy to take part. You can then ask for these at the appropriate time.
- Arrange with pupils in advance, so that they are fully briefed and prepared to take part with you.

Always treat pupils with respect. Never embarrass or belittle them on stage.

USING POEMS, STORIES AND DRAMATIC READINGS

Story-telling is one of the world's oldest forms of public communication. It is also, to this day, one of the most effective. Stories, poems and readings all create pictures with words and, since they feed rather than stifle the imagination, their potential in communicating with young people is enormous. What unites these three diverse forms is that they depend entirely for their impact on the power of the words of which they are composed. Movement, props, costumes and staging are minimal or non-existent. It is the way that the words are assembled and delivered that carries the message. These forms are useful because they lend themselves to situations in which time, space, personnel and equipment are limited. However, the dependence on word power demands a high level of practice, preparation, delivery skills and concentration.

Poems

Poems for school use should be drawn from the broad area known as performance poetry. They do not have to rhyme but they do have to have rhythm: a poem which is written or performed without respect for the rhythm of words will simply not work. In general, short, funny, topical poems will work better than long descriptive pieces. They can be used to season an assembly which also uses stories and a talk, or they can be grouped together to form an assembly in their own right.

Stories

Stories can cover anything from biblical incidents retold or modernised, through true-life stories to modern-day fictions. The parable is a very effective form of story for school use, with good characterisation and descriptions, plenty of humour and a twist in the tail.

Dramatic readings

Dramatic readings fall somewhere between a story and a sketch. They may require more than one voice. They need to have a good flow, frequent voice changes and a punchy ending. They have enormous potential for school use and particularly for involving Christian young people in assemblies since they do not require lines to be learnt or costumes and movement to be mastered. Since our culture has moved its interest largely away from radio and toward films and television, much of the scope for voice plays has remained undeveloped. There is a real wealth of imagery and effectiveness to be harnessed in dramatic reading which uses words to convey action, character and message. With lively, articulate voices and adequate rehearsal the potential to captivate an assembly audience with the equivalent of a three-minute radio play is strong.

There are five points to bear in mind when selecting material:
1　Use humour to open a way for your message. You do not have to be funny all the time, but being funny at least some of the time will help. Take great care, however, not to 'diminish' people by humour. Comedy and satire form a major part of the teenage TV diet; but an assembly piece that makes fun of other people, no matter how remote they may be from the school's life, inevitably carries an unspoken message about the way in which Christians regard and value others.
2　Be prepared to address a wide range of issues. Talk about life, the universe and everything and look for 'signposts' to the gospel. A poem, story or reading does not have to get to the foot of the cross

– nor even be explicitly Christian – in order to justify its use. Good writing is as much about observing truth and reality as it is about preaching a message.

3 Don't be afraid to raise questions as well as providing answers. Much of the value of poetry, stories and dramatic readings lies in their ability to open up the right questions rather than in their ability to offer specific answers.

4 Good quality, well written material is in short supply so experiment with writing your own and encourage the potential of friends and colleagues.

5 Test out your selection of material, where possible, with groups of young people. Learn to respect their views: if they say it isn't funny, it's because it isn't, not because they hate you!

In your preparation remember that the spaces and pauses between the words are as important as the words themselves. Professionalism is all about timing. It is essential to rehearse: practise more than once and practise out loud. Varying the pitch and tone of the voice is also very important. Practise, explore, experiment and develop.

USING DRAMA

'Let's do some drama!'
'Yes! That'll be good!'
Such enthusiam often rings hollow once the drama has been 'done' and was deemed anything but 'good'! We know that people remember what they see much longer than something they simply hear. Drama therefore, which combines the audible and the visual, is especially effective. But it can also communicate a powerful and long-lasting negative message if performed badly. The dramatist therefore needs to give as much careful thought to preparing a dramatic sketch as a good preacher does to crafting a sermon. Here are some hints on how to use drama in the school assembly.

Obey simple dramatic rules:

1 Don't turn your back to the audience.
2 Always speak clearly and slowly enough for people to hear.
3 Don't clog the narrow strip along the platform edge with ten assorted angels and a chorus.
4 Use minimum props and costumes to highlight a scene but don't let them take over.

Being professional in approach is not unspiritual, nor is it egotistic to want to do well for God.

Remember the subject

Make sure the sketch, whether parable or illustration, connects comfortably with the theme. The parable of the sower, for instance, isn't about famine! Leave people thinking (as Jesus did) about how the sketch relates to the issue or topic but make sure the audience is not left thinking simply, 'Eh?' If you base a sketch on a Bible passage, treat that passage with integrity. Don't force it to say something it never meant to.

Don't overload your material

Good assemblies make only one simple point. Even the *Reader's Digest* can't condense Luke's Gospel into three minutes! Longer sketches, up to full assembly length, are harder to prepare and perform and don't always work as well as the short, sharp shocks! Use material which says only what you *need* to say, not everything you'd like people to hear.

Don't overload your actors (or your hosts)

Think in terms of using two to four actors, not the entire cast of *Ben Hur*! The only exception to this would be if there are several Christian pupils from the school prepared to be involved. You may then be able to be more ambitious, depending on how much time and opportunity you have to rehearse and to arrange the staging. Whether with many or few actors,

familiar faces are generally much more acceptable to the audience than a handful of strangers.

Surprise them!

Assemblies are traditionally 'switch-off' points for most pupils. So don't be timid in your presentation. Many sketches designed for performance in the open air work well in schools because of their 'over the top' emphasis on movement, noise and frantic action. Wake them up before they nod off but don't frighten head teachers!

Aim to entertain

Don't get obsessed with the message and so forget the medium of entertainment. Enjoyment – which need not be simply 'funny stuff' – can be a powerful weapon in breaking down the 'religion is boring' barrier.

Be culturally relevant

Even if you may never have 'street cred' yourself, you need to know what is going on in the pupils' worlds. Your characters, situations, language and humour should relate to what's happening in their world today.

Some types of character are timeless – gangsters, pirates, detectives, aliens, for instance; but others are not. If you want to set parables or stories in the youth sub-cultures of today, you will need to check that you have the right terms!

Be creative

There are many books of excellent drama sketches on the market with material suitable for use in assemblies. Besides these, experiment yourself, using the Bible, characters, life, current or past happenings and a little imagination, to produce new sketches. Drama games and role play can also produce useful results. Many great sketches are never written down!

Use volunteers

Drama can be an excellent way for people from your church to become involved in leading assemblies. Taking part in one with other people is less threatening than having to do one single-handed but may give the confidence to do so in the future.

Suggestions for drama resources

Paul Burbridge and Murray Watts: *Laughter in Heaven*. Bromley: Marc Europe, 1985. *Lightning Sketches*. London: Hodder and Stoughton, 1981. *Red Letter Days*. London: Hodder and Stoughton, 1986. *Time to Act*. London: Hodder and Stoughton, 1979.
Steven and Janet Stickley: *Footnotes*. London: Hodder and Stoughton, 1987. *Using the Bible in Drama*. Swindon: The Bible Society, 1981.

Note:
The copyright holder's permission should always be obtained before performing any play or sketch. Most of the authors listed above have decided upon a fixed fee which grants the right to perform all the sketches in their book. Specific details are given at the front of each title.

USING AUDIO-VISUAL AIDS

A well chosen picture is worth a thousand words and a well chosen visual aid, integrated into your assembly, can greatly enhance your communication power. Here is a check list of 'dos' and 'don'ts' to help avoid the pitfalls inherent in the use of projectors and the like. Don't let the technology put you off, do read this list carefully. Learn from the mistakes of others – not your own!

Dos:

1 Do check up on the availability of all the necessary equipment:
• Does the school have the

equipment you need? There's no point in 'carrying coals to Newcastle' but beware, school equipment is often well used, jealously guarded and slightly the worse for wear.

- Are there sufficient power sockets in the hall? Will you need to take extension leads?
- Always carry a spare bulb for overhead projectors (OHPs) and film strip projectors and know how to fit it!
- Make sure that cassette players have sufficient volume and sound quality for the size of room.

2 Do enlist the help of someone to be your projectionist (for OHP or filmstrip) but make sure you know how the equipment works in case they fail to turn up.

3 Do book videos, tapes and soundstrips well in advance.

4 Do check that the audio-visual aid (AVA) you intend to use is designed for the age range that will be present at the assembly.

5 Do listen to or watch the AVA right through, preferably on the equipment to be used in the assembly, well before 'the day' so that there is time to change your plans if it is not suitable.

6 Do arrive in good time to set up the equipment. Focus projector(s) and check the sound. Make sure the chairs are set up so that everyone can see the screen.

7 Do take careful note of timings. Many AVAs are too long for use in assemblies. You need to leave time to sum up at the end and you do not want to overrun the bell at the end of the assembly.

Don'ts:

1 Don't use AVAs as entertainment or as an excuse for shoddy preparation! Plan your assembly carefully first and then choose an appropriate AVA to enhance your presentation and means of communication.

2 Don't expect your audience to listen attentively to an audio tape for more than two or three minutes.

3 Don't use taped talks which were originally delivered in a very different setting.

4 Don't forget to position cassette players/loudspeakers to achieve the best sound quality. The general rule is that the nearer the sound is to the screen the better, so don't put the cassette player next to the projector.

5 Don't use a video/TV format with more than thirty people. Use filmstrips.

6 Don't forget to check whether the pupils may have seen the AVA before (for instance in RE classes).

Sources of materials

Many organisations produce audio-visual aids. Here are the addresses of some of them. Contact them for an up-to-date catalogue of what is available.

For original material: videos and sound strips for sale or hire:
Scripture Union. 9–11 Clothier Road, Brislington, Bristol, BS4 5RL.
Church Pastoral Aid Society. Falcon Court, 32 Fleet Street, London, EC4Y 1 DB.

For videos for sale or hire:
CTVC. Hillside Studios, Merry Hill Road, Bushey, Watford, Herts. WD2 1DR.
International Films. 235 Shaftesbury Avenue, London, WC2H 8EL.

For a wide range of resource materials for hire:
Christian Resources Project. 14 Lipson Road, Plymouth, Devon. PL4 8PW.

For videos and sound strips for sale or hire on the two-thirds world:

TEAR Fund. 100 Church Road, Teddington, Middlesex. TW11 8QE.
Christian Aid. 240–250 Ferndale Road, London. SW9 8BH.

For OHP picture sequences:
Christian Publicity Organisation. Garcia Estate, Canterbury Road, Worthing, West Sussex. BN13 1BW. These picture sequences are for use as a basis to your own commentary. Particularly valuable are those on the life and witness of David Sheppard, Eric Liddell and C T Studd.

PUTTING IT ALL TOGETHER

It is useful to try to put ourselves in the shoes of the pupils to whom we will be speaking, before even thinking of the content of the assembly we will present. Try these two exercises:

First, think back to your own school days. What do you remember about the assemblies you sat through? What sort of assembly impressed you and what bored you silly? Why did some seem good and others a waste of time?

Next, try to remember the sort of thoughts that went through your mind as the person up at the front spoke. Were you worrying about not having homework ready to hand in? The 'test' later in the morning? Your girlfriend/ boyfriend sitting three rows in front? An argument you had with your mum before you came out? Maybe assembly was just a time to catch up on sleep!

Above everything else, assemblies need to be relevant and attention grabbing. If they fail on either of these counts our message, no matter how valuable in itself, will not get across. So how do we go about putting one together?

The aim and desired response

The first decision you need to make is what point you want pupils to understand and what sort of a response you can hope to encourage from them. The two must be thought out together; it is no good having an aim that cannot legitimately be responded to in the school context. For example, the aim we have stated for *Raise the Kon Tiki*? is 'To challenge pupils to consider for themselves what values they are going to live by.' In the Application and response section we invite pupils to think about the values they are choosing in life, in particular whether there may be things more valuable than personal safety and comfort.

It would have been possible to go for a much more 'evangelistic' aim in our use of the Kon Tiki story. For instance, 'To show that although Christianity may look unattractive it is actually the only way to God.' While this may be a helpful approach to take in a church youth group or youth service, its overtly evangelistic or 'dogmatic' approach would not be acceptable in the school context. The application which logically follows from this aim is, 'If you are not a Christian you are not on the right road' and the response that will be asked for will push pupils into making a decision about whether or not they will accept Christianity.

So, think carefully about the aim and desired response and about the sort of phrases you will use to get these across. (Refer back to the article, 'Setting the scene', for details.)

The opening

From the outset, we have to win the attention and respect of the pupils. We will do this only if they see immediately that the subject-matter we present is relevant. And they will be awake to realise this only if we have torn their attention away from homework, boyfriends and arguments, with an attention-grabbing opening line.

The element of surprise will usually work to your advantage in gaining attention, particularly on a first visit. One way is to start with a sketch to create a sense of anticipation among the pupils (see *The root of bitterness*) or to walk on impersonating a game show host (see *The price is right!*).

The rest of the input

Don't be afraid of using humour in getting your message across, perhaps by pointing out the absurd in life (see *Would you believe it?*) or by retelling an amusing incident (see *Missing the point*). Laughter is a great relaxer. It gets pupils on your side and will help them to be more open to what you have to say. It also helps dispel preconceived ideas about 'boring' Christians. Boring people don't have a sense of humour.

If humour is not your style you may prefer to use other arresting methods of presentation. A carefully presented dramatic monologue can create suspense and anticipation, opening the way for a thought-provoking application and response. The use of props or unusual objects (see *The slime dip*) can also be effective 'attention grabbers'. The most effective ones are those which, like *The slime dip*, actually contain your message in a visual form. Jesus used parables to create vivid pictures in people's minds which in some way paralleled the truth he wanted them to grasp. The images he gave of sheep, branches, bread, light and darkness would stick in the minds of his hearers far longer than a theoretical description of the spiritual reality.

Pupil participation is another way of stimulating and maintaining interest. See the comments on page 17 for suggestions of how to involve them.

As we give the assembly, we are perhaps the key ingredient in its success or failure. We are part of the message we present, a living visual aid for the work of Christ in our lives. It is crucial to come across as being enthusiastic about and enthused by our message; it must be something genuinely good that we want to share with the pupils. Sharing from our own experience, and the use of personal anecdotes and stories, is often vital to bring to life the point we wish to communicate.

Resources

Here are some of the places to start as you stretch out beyond the limits of *Assembly Point* to produce your own assembly outlines.

The Bible is an obvious mine of resource material. The parables of Jesus can be retold using contemporary illustrations, or you may like to write your own simple sketches or poems around biblical characters and situations. You may know colleagues or church members who, with encouragement, can loose their creative abilities on your behalf.

Almost anything of current interest can be commented on from a distinctively Christian perspective – much as Jesus used current events and everyday situations to help explain something about God and his relationship with people (see, for example, Luke 5:29–31; 6:46–49; 7:6–10; 13:1–5; Matthew 5:14–16; 8:18–20). Newspapers and magazines provide a virtually endless supply of human interest stories that can be used to good effect here. It is important that what we say is seen to be relevant to the world in which the young people find themselves, and shows that the Christian faith helps make sense of that world.

It is worth collecting books of Christian poetry and drama sketches, as suggested in earlier articles in this book. A trip to W H Smith may also be most productive. Some of our favourite anecdotes are gleaned from books like: *The Book of Heroic Failures*, by S Pile (Macdonald Futura), *Famous Last Words*, by J Green (Pan), *It Can't be True*, by J Reid (St Michael), *The Book of Facts*, by I Asimov (Coronet) and, of course, *The Guinness Book of Records*.

Section three of this book gives you a start in collecting your own resource material. We have deliberately not suggested ways of using the items there so that you have a free hand to use them in whatever way you feel most appropriate to your assemblies.

Part Two

READY-MADE ASSEMBLY OUTLINES

Truth and ultimate values

RAISE THE 'KON TIKI'?

Introduction

Aim:
To challenge pupils to consider for themselves what values they are going to live by.

Preparation:
You will need to retell the story below. You could do so by working it into a sketch with three players: one person on the *Kon Tiki*, one on the *Titanic*, and yourself as narrator. Alternatively, you could re-write it as a dramatic reading to be read by three people. In either case you will need minimal props – something for each actor to sit on and two large notices to be displayed at the end of the sketch saying, 'Kon Tiki' and 'Titanic'. The characters can be male or female; change the wording of the script below to whatever is more appropriate for your actors.

Content

'There is a clear blue sky and a calm blue sea. On the sea floats a raft. It's not much of a sailing craft, just logs tied together, with what looks like a garden shed on top. A rough mast has been erected with a tattered bedsheet for a sail. A man sits on the edge of the raft, humming to himself. He is untidy with ragged jeans, torn vest and stubbly chin. Across the ocean he can see a huge liner powering its way towards him.

On the deck of the liner sits a well-dressed, well-brought-up, well-drunk man. He is sunbathing in a deck chair and sipping dry martinis when suddenly his attention is drawn to the raft now bobbing within hailing distance of the liner. The man in the deck chair gets up and leans on the ship's rail to shout to the man on the raft.

'Ahoy there! You OK?'
'Oh, hello. Didn't see you up there. How are you?'
'I'm fine – but how are *you*? That's rather more the point!'
'Oh, I'm great!'
'Well, can't we rescue you, or something?'
'Rescue me? No, thank you very much.'
'Your raft looks terribly dangerous – and so cramped! Why don't you come up here? Look at this liner – isn't it a beauty? 242 cabins, five swimming pools, three ice rinks, four racing stables, two eighteen-hole golf courses, the Hilton Hotel. . .'
'No thanks, I'm OK here. (*Pause*). Actually, I think *you're* the one who needs rescuing!
'What? Don't be silly!'

The man on the raft now proceeds to try to convince the man on the liner that he would be better off on the raft. (You will need to script this yourself.)

Stop the story after a few moments and take a vote. Ask the assembly how many, if they had to choose, would rather be on the raft and how many would prefer the liner. Experience is that the vast majority go for the liner!

Back to the story. The two keep trying to convince one another that each would be better off on the other's boat, but neither budges. In the end the two boats begin to sail apart.

'As the man on the liner looks down onto the raft he sees two words cut into the logs. The two words are (*person on raft turns round notice*) "Kon Tiki."

As the man on the raft looks up at the liner rapidly disappearing towards the horizon, he notices one word written in large letters on its stern. The word is (*person on liner turns round notice*) "Titanic." '

Briefly explain what the *Kon Tiki* and the *Titanic* were: The *Kon Tiki* was made of balsa logs lashed together with rope. It took four men 4,200 miles across the Pacific Ocean, carried by currents, from the coast of Peru to the Polynesian islands. The whole journey took 97 days. The *Titanic*, however, was a British liner, said to be unsinkable. But, on the night of 14–15 April 1912, it struck an iceberg in the North Atlantic and sunk. The disaster, which occurred on the ship's maiden voyage, claimed the lives of more than 1,500 of the 2,200 people on board.

Then take the vote again asking who, in the light of what they know now, think they would sooner be on the raft and who on the liner.

Hopefully you will find that some have changed their minds since the first vote.

Application and response

Draw out the point of the story in a way such as the following:

'You may believe that the way to get the most out of life is to live in luxury with all the Pepsi, chocolate cake, CDs and swimming pools you could want. That seems a very attractive proposition. In contrast, it looks very risky and perhaps a bit stupid to choose a different set of values and live a different sort of life. After all, it's far safer to stick with the crowd – isn't it?'

Add in an example from your personal experience of a time when, because of your Christian beliefs, you decided to do something very different – and a bit risky – from what everyone else around you was doing. Alternatively, give an example of a famous historical or present-day Christian, such as Lord Shaftesbury or Mother Teresa. Draw out that they decided to live their lives according to values Christians think are important. It cost them a lot, but they may well have gained much more than those who risked nothing because they were more concerned about personal safety and comfort.

IT DOESN'T MATTER WHAT YOU BELIEVE!

Introduction

Aim:
To destroy the myth that it doesn't matter what you believe as long as you believe in something.

Preparation:
The assembly runs as a conversation between you and one or more pupils that you invite onto the platform (see point 8, page 17).

You will need a table and chair on the platform for yourself.

You will also need a packet of each of the following (or similar) which should be hidden in a box or bag and brought out as required: Sugar Puffs; bird seed; Go-Cat; blood, bone and fishmeal fertilizer; Polyfilla and a bowl and spoon.

Content

Sit at the table, facing the audience. Those pupils taking part could already be on stage, chatting or 'working'. Alternatively, invite them up now.

Compose a talk along these lines:

'You know, some people say it doesn't matter **what** you believe as long as you believe something. (Pause.)

While you're thinking about that I hope you'll excuse me but I had to get up early this morning to take your assembly – I hope you don't mind if I have my breakfast now. (Tip some Sugar Puffs into the bowl and eat a few. Then turn to pupils on stage.)

Do you like Sugar Puffs? Have you all had breakfast this morning? No? Oh dear – it's important to eat; you won't grow strong and healthy if you don't eat. Well, it's your lucky day today. I've got a choice for you. Come and have a look.

Are you feeling a bit peckish? I've got just the thing. (Produce and hold up bird seed.) How about a nice bowl full of this? How's your singing this morning? It will be top notch after eating this! . . . No? (Stand packet on table.)

Perhaps you need something a bit more substantial. (Produce Go-Cat.) Listen to this. (Read appropriate blurb from packet, eg vitamins and minerals for extra energy.) That will come in handy if you've got games or PE today! . . . No?

What about something to help you grow? This is ideal. (Produce fertilizer.) This is made out of dried blood, rotten fish heads and dried up bones. Stick your finger in and try a bit! (Allow time for reaction!)

(To volunteers) What lessons have you got this morning? Maths? You need something really solid inside you to see you through that. How about a nice bowl of Polyfilla? (Produce packet.) Just think – a good solid lump of this inside your stomach will keep you going through maths. . . No? You're rather hard to please!

(With frustration) Listen, it doesn't matter *what* you eat as long as you eat *something*! (Turn to audience.) Isn't that true? (Pause.)'

Turn to participants, thank them for their help and ask them to go back to their places.

Application and response

'We would think someone silly who said that it doesn't matter what you eat, as long as you eat something. But some people say it doesn't matter what you *believe*, so long as you believe in something.

But it does matter what you believe, because what you believe will affect the way you live. You might believe it was right to murder people – but would that be a right belief?

We need to eat the right things to stay physically healthy. Perhaps we need to believe the right things to be spiritually healthy.'

HEADS, YOU WIN!

Introduction

Aim:
To encourage pupils to think about the purpose of life.

Preparation:
You will need each of the four heads shown on page 35 on separate OHP acetates.

Content

Ask for four volunteers from the assembly. Preferably get people who have a reputation for having plenty to say for themselves (see point 8 on page 17). Ask the assembly to imagine that they are all aliens from another star system hovering above the earth in their space-craft. They have beamed up the four 'volunteers' as representative human beings to ask them what are the most important things in life to human beings. Each 'human being' has to pinpoint the most important thing, in just one sentence.

At the end of the final speech the aliens must vote on who they agree with most.

Thank the four earth-dwellers and ask them to go back to their seats. Explain that all of us carry our own ideas of what is most important in life. Proceed to show in turn the different 'heads' that people choose. For example, display the 'heart' face and talk about how one group of people might choose to believe that relationships/sex/marriage is what makes for a fulfilled life. Do the same for each. Explain as you go that although many of these things might be good, they might also leave us very disappointed, and even hurt.

Application and response

Explain that as a Christian you believe there is more to life than any of those heads suggest. Switch off the OHP, and continue: 'When Jesus Christ was asked to pinpoint the most important thing in life, his answer didn't have anything to do with jobs, money, status, sex or possessions. This is what he said: "Love the Lord your God with all your heart and with all your soul and with all your mind. This is the first and greatest commandment." (Matthew 22:37, 38)

Jesus was saying that it is possible to know God personally – even to love him and to be loved by him, and that this is what matters most in life.'

Ask the pupils to spend a few moments in silence, and to think how they would have answered that question; 'What is the most important thing in life?'

Money

Music

Socialising

Relationships

SIX YEARS AND FIFTY MILES LATER...

Introduction

Aim:
To show that some things are so important that they deserve our total commitment.

Preparation:
You will need to prepare some extracts from the *Guinness Book of Records*, which show how some people have put an enormous amount of time, energy and dedication into achieving things that are not of much worth in themselves.

Content

Begin by reading out your three or four prepared extracts from the *Guinness Book of Records*.

Go on to comment that we might not think it was really worth all that effort, just to see who could eat the most hard-boiled eggs, play tiddlywinks for longest, or whatever. In fact, if a person was always doing this sort of thing and never, for instance, enjoying friendships, we might begin to think they'd got their priorities wrong.

Here's a story about one girl who ought to be in the *Guinness Book of Records*. She discovered that there was a book which contained some very important things, and she badly wanted a copy of it.

'Mary Jones was born over two hundred years ago in a tiny hamlet in North Wales called Ty'n-ddol. Her parents were weavers but they were very poor. Each Sunday Mary and her parents would go to the chapel and would listen to the minister reading from the Bible. Mary tried to remember as much as she could as Welsh Bibles were scarce and usually cost a lot of money and neither Mary nor her parents had had the opportunity to learn to read.

Mary longed to be able to read – and particularly to read from the Bible. Then one day word came to the village that a school was going to start so that the children could learn to read. It was held in the chapel and Mary learnt quickly and made such good progress that one day she was allowed to stand up in the chapel and read from the Bible.

From that day Mary decided that she would save up and buy a Bible of her own, even if it took years – and it did! By doing jobs in the village she earned small sums of money and it took her six years to collect enough. She was now fifteen years old.

Unfortunately there was not one Welsh Bible for sale anywhere in or near her home village. She was told that she would have to go and see Mr Charles, the minister who had taught her to read. He lived in the town of Bala which was about twenty-five miles away. It was a journey Mary would have to make on foot to see if she could buy a Bible but she was undaunted and, after getting her parents' permission, she set out for Bala.

When she reached Bala there was another disappointment. Mr Charles had sold all his Bibles and would not be receiving any more from London for some time. However, when he saw her disappointment and heard her story he felt he could not refuse her the thing she wanted most in the world. He had one Welsh Bible which had been promised to a friend who he knew would understand. Mary returned home with the Bible she had struggled so hard to obtain.

She had learned to read, saved up for six years and walked to a town miles away from her home in order that she could read her own Bible! And her commitment had other results too. The story of Mary Jones led to the setting up of the Bible Society in London to make the Bible available to people throughout the world in their own language and at a price they could afford.'

Application and response

'Today it's easy to read a Bible if we want to. Some people will have one at home, or read one in school. Or we can go to W H Smith's and buy one. But in some countries Bibles are still rare and some people believe it is so important to them to read what it says about God and the world that they save up, travel for miles, and even risk imprisonment and death in order to get a Bible.

For us, so many things compete for our time and attention that we sometimes have to ask ourselves what the really important things are in our lives.

What do you think are the most important things to be committed to and to spend time thinking about?'

(Note: A fuller account of the story of Mary Jones is available in a booklet by June Bosanquet, published by the Bible Society, Stonehill Green, Westlea, Swindon, SN5 7DG.)

MISSING THE POINT

Introduction

Aim:
To show that we can easily get the wrong idea about Christianity, simply because we have already decided what it's all about before really investigating it.

Content

Introduce the assembly with the thought that sometimes we can misunderstand what is being said to us and jump to completely the wrong conclusions. This can totally change the meaning and so we miss the point of what is being said to us. Read out the following, keeping a straight face. (Please note: if you have any doubts about this causing offence in some schools, do not use this outline. Our experience is, however, that the story is usually very well received; often teachers will come to us afterwards and ask us for copies!)

'Did you hear about the English lady who wanted to buy a house in a remote village in Switzerland? On her return home she realised that she didn't see the toilet in her new house. So she wrote to the Swiss estate agent asking about the location of the WC. The estate agent had very little knowledge of the English language and so asked the parish priest to translate the letter for him. The only meaning for 'WC' that he could think of was 'Wayside Chapel.' This is therefore the reply received by the English lady.

'My Dear Madam,
I take great pleasure in informing you that the WC is situated nine miles from the house in the centre of a beautiful grove of pine trees surrounded by lovely grounds.

It is capable of holding 229 people and it is open on Sundays and Thursdays only. As there are a great number of people expected during the summer months, it is an unfortunate situation, especially if you are in the habit of going regularly. It may interest you to know that my daughter was married in the WC and it was there that she met her husband. I can remember the rush there was for seats. There were ten people to every seat usually occupied by one.

You will be glad to hear that a good number of people bring their lunch and make a day of it, while those who can afford to go by car arrive just in time. I would especially recommend your ladyship to go on Thursdays when there is an organ accompaniment. The acoustics are excellent, even the most delicate sounds can be heard everywhere.

The newest addition is a bell donated by a wealthy resident of the district. It rings every time a person enters. A bazaar is to be held to provide plush seats for all, since the people feel it is long needed. My wife is rather delicate and she cannot attend regularly. It is almost a year since she went last, and naturally it pains her very much not to be able to go more often.

I shall be delighted to reserve the best

seat for you, where you shall be seen by all. For the children, there is a special day and time so that they do not disturb the elders. Hoping to be of some service to you.

Yours faithfully.'

Application and response

'Sometimes when we hear words like "God", "Bible", "Jesus", and "Christianity" we can often associate them with words like "boring", "irrelevant", "stupid", "just for old ladies". But do our reactions spring from a real understanding of what these words describe?'

From personal experience briefly share that words like 'God' and 'Bible' have deep meaning for you, and how your knowledge of these things has influenced your life, attitudes and the way you view the world. Explain that millions of Christians today would testify that these words *actually* describe 'peace', 'hope', 'love' and 'freedom'.

Suggest that many people dismiss the claims of the Christian faith as a mistake, fable or fiction without stopping to examine the evidence too closely. Leave them with this thought: 'If you have always thought that Christianity was boring and out-of-date, perhaps you have a mistaken idea of what it's all about.'

PUTTING BELIEF INTO ACTION

Introduction

Aim:
To show that there is a difference between believing something and letting a belief change you.

Preparation:
It is best to tell the story in your own words, presenting it as dramatically as possible. (Note: we discovered several variations of the story and some of the details are shrouded in legend. However this is the version we believe to be most reliable!)

Content

'Charles Blondin was one of the world's greatest funambulists (that's a tightrope walker to you and me), and on September 15th 1860 he performed one of the most amazing stunts the world has ever seen. Blondin, before a great crowd, walked a tightrope stretched across Niagara Falls in Canada. The tightrope was 160 feet above the falls and it stretched for 1100 feet across. Amazingly, he did it!

After he had walked one way he asked the crowd if they believed he could carry a person back with him. They all shouted 'Yes!' because he was the greatest tightrope walker in the world. So he then asked for a volunteer – but no one spoke up! No one was prepared to trust Blondin and put what they believed into practice. But eventually one person did agree to go. He was Henry Colcord, Blondin's manager. He alone had real confidence and trust in Blondin's skill as a tightrope walker.'

Application and response

'The crowd in this story all said they believed in the abilities of Blondin but when he challenged them to do something about it, for someone to trust him to carry them across, no-one moved. They weren't prepared to put their beliefs into action.

Every day people say they believe in things but are these beliefs important enough to them to act on them? Many people say they believe in God but the Bible also talks about having *faith* in God. Being a Christian is more than just believing in God, it's trusting him with the whole of one's life.'

Give an illustration from your own Christian experience to show what putting your faith in God has meant to you. Then suggest the following.

'In a few moments of quietness, think about the belief you have about God. If you think your belief is true, how does it affect the way you live?'

THE PARABLE OF THE BLOWER

Introduction

Aim:
To encourage pupils to respond to what they hear about God.

Preparation:
You will need several round balloons for the assembly. Ask each of your helpers to blow up a balloon but not to tie a knot in it. (You will need at least one of them uninflated so pretend you cannot blow yours up unless someone else is clearly having trouble.)

Content

Compose a talk along these lines:
1   (Hold up the uninflated balloon.) 'Some people are just like this first balloon. I don't mean that they're red (or whatever colour it happens to be) and that you can pull them about, but that nothing you tell them ever goes in.
2   Some people are like this balloon. (Take hold of an inflated balloon.) Again I don't mean that they are round and yellow, but when they listen to information it doesn't stay with them for very long, and quickly disappears. (Let go of the balloon so that it shoots off round the hall.)
3   Other people are like this balloon. (Take another inflated balloon. Stretch its lips between your forefingers and thumbs so that it makes a screeching noise.

Speak between making the noise.) What they hear goes in . . . but it doesn't stay for very long . . . and gradually . . . they forget all about what was said . . . until they end up just like the first balloon.
4   Some people however are just like this last balloon. (Take the final inflated balloon and tie a knot in it so that none of the air escapes.) What they hear goes in, but not only does it go in but it stays. They act on what they hear and everyone can see the difference it makes to them.'

Application and response

Explain that the illustration helps us to understand how people respond when they hear about God:
   'Some people, no matter what they hear about God, reject it instantly. "God doesn't exist" they say.
   Other people hear about God and think, "Well, he's OK for religious people." They don't bother to think any more about it so quickly forget what they heard.
   Still others are really interested when they hear about God – for a while. But then lots of other things have to be done: there's the telly to watch, discos to go to . . . things just crowd God out and they slowly forget about him.
   Others, when they hear about him, listen and think carefully. →

Some of these people discover that he can really make a difference to their lives.'

Speak from your own experience to show how responding to God has changed your life. Alternatively, use some of the quotes below to illustrate how some well-known people have responded to God and found that he has changed their lives.

- Glen Hoddle, footballer: 'I've got an inner peace and a strength and a strong faith in God.'
- Mother Teresa speaks of her sense of total security in God's hands: 'What is the Good News, the Gospel? That God loves you, that God carries you tattooed on the palms of his hands, that even if a mother should forget her own child God will not forget you.'
- Wendy Craig, actress: 'I feel a different person inside; much more positive and safe . . . more on an even keel now.'

→

- Steve McQueen, actor: 'I expect to win my battle against cancer, but no matter how it goes, I'm at peace with God, I can't lose.'
- Bobby Ball, of 'Cannon and Ball': 'For years I thought I was happy, but the more money I got – the more angry I got. I started getting into fights and messing up my life. I looked for God but I didn't find him – not until a Chaplain in Bradford told me to get down on my knees and ask God for forgiveness. I did just that and I didn't stop crying for three days.

People take the mickey now, but I'm not bothered. He's changed my life and helps me through every day. It's funny, isn't it! I've made enough money to buy anything I want, but the greatest thing we can have, God's love in our lives, comes free – and ninety per cent of us don't want it!'

End with the challenge, 'How are you responding to what you hear about God?'

Encouraging a sense
of self worth

LOSERS?

Introduction

Aim:
To encourage pupils with the affirmation that God has time for 'losers'.

Preparation:
You will not need any props but you will need to think carefully beforehand about how you are going to fill out the outline below with your own personal anecdotes.

Content

'For every winner there is a loser. For every gold medal winner there are hundreds of failures. For every band at Number one there are hundreds who don't make it. For every *Meatloaf* there is a *Currant Bun* and for every *Wet Wet Wet* there is a *Drip Drip Drip* (substitute contemporary groups).

We often feel sorry for losers, eg at Wimbledon or in the FA Cup Final. (Add personal anecdotes here about your dreams of being on the winning side.)'

Here are the stories of three losers.

Loser 1: In 1970 a lion escaped from a circus in Italy. Typically, it found a small boy and started to chase him. Less typically, the small boy's mother turned on the lion and badly mauled it. The animal suffered severe head and skin wounds and received treatment for shock.

Loser 2: One winter's day, a man got his lips frozen to his car door whilst blowing on the iced-up lock trying to defrost it. He earned himself the nickname, 'Hot Lips'.

Loser 3: For twenty years Mr Geoffrey O'Neill has been writing what he calls 'good catchy tunes that people remember and whistle.' In this time he has composed 501 songs and three musicals. Not one of them has been recorded, published or performed by professionals.

Mr O'Neill files all his songs away in case there should be a sudden demand for them. He cheerfully reports that song number 102 is called, 'Try, Try Again', while number 332 is entitled, 'People Think I'm Stupid'. An oil firm employee, he gives public lectures on how unsuccessful his songs are.

(Taken from *The Book of Heroic Failures*, by Stephen Pile. London: Macdonald Futura, 1979.)

Application and response

'We may know loads of losers – we may even feel that we are one. Christians believe that Jesus lived to demonstrate what God is like. Here is a story from the New Testament that shows how Jesus responded to losers.'

Read or tell the story of Blind Bartimaeus, Mark 10:46–52.

'That blind beggar found that when he called out to Jesus, Jesus didn't ignore him. It's great to know that God has time for losers, because that means we can know that he will always have time for us.'

THE PRICE IS RIGHT

Introduction

Aim:
To show that each person is very valuable to God.

Preparation:
The assembly takes on the character of a TV game show. You will need to be prepared to imitate a game show host (à la Lesley Crowther – loads of false grins, empty jollity and OTT humour!). You will also need:

- Eight containers (empty jam jars will do – a rack of test tubes would be ideal). Each should be part or wholly filled with a chemical-looking substance, such as unmixed Polyfilla or talcum powder.
- A dummy microphone.
- An OHP acetate or large sheet of card bearing the list of ingredients below.
- An item that you know the value of, eg your radio, earrings, wellies – anything that you can carry in to the assembly.
- Eight small prizes, such as *Milky Way* bars.

Before the assembly you will also need to ask the teacher in charge for the names of eight pupils who would be prepared to appear in your 'Game Show'.

Content

Go straight into host role and welcome everyone to your show: 'The Price is Right'. Explain the rules of the show. Four people have been randomly selected by computer to come to the front to guess the value of certain objects. The person who guesses nearest to the true value is the winner.

Call up your first group of four contestants, show them the item which you have brought and give each person the chance to guess the value and write it on a card. Then ask each in turn to reveal their guess to the 'studio audience'. Build up the excitement as you announce the true value and reveal the winner. Give each contestant a small prize.

Call up the next four contestants and reveal the collection of 'chemicals'. Display the OHP or card showing the list of ingredients and ask for each contestant to make their guess as to what they are worth in total and to write it down, as before.

Reveal the real cost (eg £7.13), applaud the winner and reward the contestants.

Come out of character and explain the significance of that particular set of chemicals: every human being contains this set of chemicals. Each of us has:

FAT enough for seven bars of soap
IRON enough for one medium-sized nail
SUGAR enough for seven cups of tea
LIME enough to whitewash one chicken coop

PHOSPHORUS enough to tip 2,100 matches
MAGNESIUM enough for one dose of salts
POTASH enough to explode one toy crane
SULPHUR enough to rid one dog of fleas

Application and response

'Is that all we are worth? Just £7.13? If we knew slaves were being sold for £7.13 we'd be disgusted that human life could be valued so cheaply. Perhaps, at times, people do put us down and make us feel valueless. Parents and "friends" can sometimes make us feel like no one cares; no one would pay 7p for us, never mind £7!

But there's some good news. Although we might sometimes feel worthless, unloved and unvalued, God always thinks we're great! He sometimes hates the things we *do* but He always loves *us*. He knows our bodies are only chemicals but he loves the real us inside, our personality.

Here are some verses from the Bible, written by someone when he realised that God really did love him very much. (Read Psalm 103:13–17.)

I'm going to close by reading a prayer. Listen quietly to the words and if you want to make them your own say "Amen" with me at the end.

"Father God, thank you that although you know that our bodies are just made up of cheap chemicals you love us. When we are feeling worthless and put down by other people, help us to remember that you will always love us. Amen." '

THE BALLAD OF JESSE AND JAKE

Introduction

Aim:
To show that each person is unique and special to God.

Preparation:
You will need someone to share the leading of this assembly with you.

Content

The first person should introduce the assembly by stating that every person is different. Everyone is a unique individual, we've been made that way. . .

If there is time, the second person could read the poem, 'Unique' (see page 95).

The first person continues with a talk along these lines. . .

'Each of us is unique. Some of us have fair hair, some dark hair; some like maths, some don't like maths; some of us like macaroni cheese, others prefer boiled eggs with jam. (Add other likes/dislikes, eg pop groups.)

And those are just the things we can see! If we included all the things nobody sees – the way you feel, the dreams you dream, the person you want to be, the things you're good at, no matter how many things we included, we would still have a collection of totally unique, special individuals.

You're a "one-off," every one of you.

You might look like a crowd, but a crowd is made up of individuals, just as a snowdrift looks like one big lump but is actually made up of thousands and thousands of separate crystal flakes. Every snowflake is different from every other one, and so is every person in a crowd.

You are unique. That's the way you were made and the good news in this assembly is that *God loves you just as you are.* Jesus told a story to illustrate this. Here's a more modern version of it.' (The Ballad of Jesse and Jake is now read by both people in cowboy style and accents.)

1: Once upon a time, in the days when the west was won, and a man's best friend was his horse. . .

2: There was a rancher who had two sons, Jesse and Jake.

1: One day Jesse, the younger son, came to his father and said:

2: Dad, I'm tired of workin' on this ranch and livin' with you: I wish you was dead so's I could have my share of your money now. I want to get out and make my way in the world. . .

1: So his Dad said, OK, Son, if that's what you want. . . And he divided his money between Jesse and Jake, and gave them each their pile.

2: Jake, the elder son said, thanks Dad, and went back to work. But Jesse, the younger son said: yeeeehah!

1: Yeeeeeeeehah! He said, now that I've got some money of ma' own, I can go and make ma' way in the world. . .

2: And away he went.

1: He went straight to the local saloon and bought everybody a drink: so he had lots of friends.

2: Then he got bored of the local saloon and headed for Sin City: the meanest, drinkinest, fightinest, shootinest town in the whole wild West!

1: And for a while Jesse was the meanest, drinkinest, fightinest, shootin' est son of a gun in the whole town. . .

2: Until he had spent all his money on drinking, gambling and wild living.

1: He was hung over, worn out,

2: And broke.

1: And none of the friends he'd had when he was buying the drinks wanted to talk to him.

2: So he got himself a job, at the biggest ranch in town.

1: But times were hard, and the only job they could give him was feeding the pigs.

2: And they had a lot of pigs.

1: He had to feed them, live with them, sleep with them.

2: Pretty soon he began to smell like them.

1: And the pay was terrible: he could barely afford to eat.

2: He got so low, he was even tempted to eat some of the pigs' food.

1: But they wouldn't let him, 'cause by this time he smelt even *worse* than them.

2: He was about as low as a man can get. . .

1: Then he came to his senses.

2: Not before time!

1: He thought to himself: the cow hands on my father's ranch have more to eat than this: even the guy who feeds the pigs is better off than I am. I know, I'll go back to my father and say 'Dad, I've been a dumb, stupid idiot, and I don't figure you'd want to have me as your son: but if I was a real good boy from now on . . . would you give me a job?'

2: So he got up, said goodbye to the pigs, and headed for home.

1: He was just practising his speech in his head, getting close to home, when his father saw him coming. He ran out to meet him, and gave him a great big bear hug: even though he smelt worse than the pigs!

2: He said to his father: 'Dad, I've been a dumb, stupid idiot, and I don't figure you'd want to have me as your son: but if I was a real good boy from now on . . . would you give me a job?'

1: But his dad said, No.

2: He said, No?

1: He said no, I won't give you a job: but I will welcome you back as my son. And tonight we'll have the biggest party this town has ever seen, 'cause you was dead and now you're back to life: you was lost, and now I've found you! But son, he said, would you do just one thing for me before the party starts?

2: Sure, Dad, he said, what's that?

1: Would you go into the house and have a good long bath?

Application and response

'How do you feel about the way *that* Dad loved his son? (Leave a short pause for reflection.) Jesus said that's just how God loves you.'

THE ROOT OF BITTERNESS

Introduction

Aim:
To show that lack of forgiveness makes life bitter.

Preparation:
Two people are needed for the sketch. A romantic couple are sitting in a restaurant, being very 'sloppy' over the table. Soft soppy music adds to the atmosphere.

Content

Man: That was nice.

Lady: Yes, it was lovely, especially the escargots.

Man: Personally, I loved the vol-au-vents.

Lady: Puddings.

Man: Sorry?

Lady: They were Yorkshire puddings.

Man: Oh well, whatever they were, I just love being with you, Humple Dumps. Thank you for taking me out for a meal.

Lady: Well that's all right, Hunky Dunk; one day you may be able to treat me.

Man: Yes, one day maybe, if my accountant will let me.
(The couple need to imagine a man walking past them and sitting at the other side of the restaurant).

Man: I know him.

Lady: Who?

Man: Him.

Lady: Who him?

Man: Him there.

Lady: Him where?

Man: Over there.

Lady: What about him?

Man: I know his grandfather.

Lady: His grandfather?

Man: And his grandfather knows my grandfather.

Lady: And?

Man: And his father knows my father.

Lady: And you know him?

Man: Well yes, only. . .

Lady: Yes?

Man: Our families haven't been speaking to each other for the past three generations.

Lady: Why ever not?

Man: (Shouting at imaginary man) Excuse me.

Lady: Please don't start anything.

Man: You stay out of this, this is family business Lucinda.
(Shouts) Listen you! (pause) I'm going to ask you the question that my grandfather asked your grandfather, and my father asked your father. OK? . . . And this time we want satisfaction! Right. . . WHEN ARE YOU GOING TO GIVE US BACK OUR SMARTIES?

Application and response

'Have you ever had an argument with your brother or sister, or your best friend? It might have been over something really small and unimportant but you haven't spoken to each other for days. Who does it hurt? It probably hurts your friend but it also hurts you! →

There's a story in the Bible about one of Jesus' disciples coming to him and saying, "How many times have I got to forgive someone who does wrong things against me? Should I forgive him seven times?" He probably thought that was a lot but Jesus said that he should should forgive seventy times seven. In other words, Jesus was saying there should be no limit to our forgiveness. He knew how important it is to forgive; if we don't, bitterness will mess up our lives and other people's. Staying bitter against someone doesn't do *them* any harm, but it does do *us* a lot of harm.

We'll take a few moments now to think: Is there someone that you've got a grudge against and need to forgive?'

What Christians believe

THE HOPE BULB

Introduction

Aim:
To suggest that the Bible is a book that is worth exploring.

Preparation:
You will need to prepare:
- a poster or OHP acetate, as shown below;
- an ordinary light bulb in a box bearing the words 'HOPE BULB';
- an imitation set of instructions inside the box.

You will also need the help of one pupil during the assembly (see point 8 on page 17).

Content

Mention a few discoveries or inventions that have made life easier and more pleasant. Ask people to try to imagine what life would be like without such things as washing machines; micro chips; oven chips; television; telephone; etc.

Ask the pupils for suggestions of the single most important discovery or invention ever made. It's likely that someone will say 'electricity', but, if they don't, introduce it yourself. (If they are not a very forthcoming group be ready with ideas and suggestions to lead up to 'electricity').

Explain that although electricity is a marvellous invention, today you have brought in to the school the most amazing up-to-the-minute discovery. Hold up the box and take out the incredible 'HOPE BULB'.

Ask for a volunteer to come up and hold the bulb in his right hand and then to raise his hand in the air. Tell him to close his eyes and hope hard to get the bulb to light up. When it doesn't work, ask half the audience to close their eyes and hope with the volunteer, while the other half watch the bulb light up. (Keep trying for as long as it is entertaining but don't overplay this bit and don't embarrass the volunteer.)

Pretend to be disappointed and say, 'Well, I don't know what went wrong – perhaps we should have read the instructions before using it.'

Take the 'instructions' out of the box and read:

'Secure bulb into light socket in the usual way. Turn on the light switch and hope that you have not just purchased a broken light bulb.'

Apologise – in an embarrassed sort of way – for having misled them.

Application and response

'You see how silly I looked because I didn't read the instructions and yet lots of people go through life just relying on hope. They hope that everything will turn out all right. They hope that they are →

making the right decisions. They hope that they will find happiness in a job, or in a marriage or in owning a house or a flash car.

As a Christian I don't have to just hope about a lot of these things because I've explored the Bible and believe that in it God has given me some instructions to help me make sense of life.

If God is the ultimate inventor of life, he knows how it works best. Loads of machines come with a label on the box: *"For best results follow the maker's instructions"* and
→

if God is the maker of life we should follow *his* instructions for how to live it. To do anything else would be like trying to make our new CD player work by using the instructions that came with the dishwasher!

Christians believe that God's instructions are recorded in a book called the Bible and that the Bible is God's Basic Instructions for the Best Life for Everyone (display poster).

Whose instructions for life are *you* following?"

The Bible: God's...
Basic
Instructions for the
Best
Life for
Everyone

THE GOD FOOD GUIDE

Introduction

Aim:
To encourage pupils to read the Bible for themselves.

Preparation:
You will need the following visual aids:
- (a) a box-file covered or marked to look like a big Bible with the following items inside it:
  - milk – (a pint bottle looks best but beware of spillages)
  - meat – (a tin of Spam usually raises a laugh)
  - honey – (a pot)
- (b) A pile of unopened envelopes of assorted shapes and sizes.

Content

Produce the pile of envelopes and explain that you had to leave home in a rush that morning and didn't have time to open your post. Ask if they mind you opening your letters now before assembly really gets under way.

Work your way through the pile of post making guesses at what each envelope may contain. Make out that you believe each envelope carries some good or important news (appropriate to the size and shape of the envelope) but do not open the envelope – just put it back on the pile.

For example, pick up a small pink envelope and explain that it's from your friend/fiancé/wife/ husband. You've been expecting a letter because they've been away for a while but are due back soon and this letter probably gives the date of their return.

Next, pick up a long brown envelope which, by its postmark, you guess to be from the hospital. The letter that you're waiting for is giving results of X-rays that you had recently and which may result in you having to have an operation. And so on.

Continue with something along these lines:

'It's daft having important letters that you don't open. Yet many people live with a really vital "letter" which they never open. It's called the Bible and Christians believe it's an important letter from God.

Lots of people in Britain today know next to nothing about the Bible because they have made up their minds that it is a big, black book (show visual aid) which is incredibly old-fashioned and boring. So if they've got a copy at all, they've pushed it into a dusty corner of the house and forgotten all about it.

But that's an absolute clanger! The Bible claims that you can't get on without it. Life without the Bible is only half what it's meant to be. It's like trying to live on half the calories and vitamins and proteins that you're meant to eat.

(Produce bottle of milk from inside "Bible".) Where would we be now if we hadn't guzzled lashings of *milk* when we were babies? If you think about it, mother's milk is the only 100% natural food that we can get. But the latest milk adverts try to cash in on the natural value of cow's milk as well . . . *"Enjoy a natural pinta"*, that is, it's healthy, it's good for you, it helps you to grow.

The Bible describes itself as spiritual milk which makes us grow into spiritually healthy people. It talks about the love and the life of Jesus and shows how we can start growing his attitudes in us.

It also describes itself as *meat* (produce Spam). Meat is one of the foods that builds muscle! The Bible claims to show us God's way to become strong inside, in our feelings, attitudes and emotions.

For example, it shows us how to tell the truth and forgive people and be a good friend, as Jesus was. Now to live the way of Jesus takes real guts. Any weakling can lie and swear and let people down; to be a beefy Jesus-person, with moral strength and courage, you need the meat of the Bible to help and advise you.

And when you get inside the Bible, you find that it's not a nasty taste, because the Bible is like *honey* (produce pot). If you've got a sweet tooth, you'll have a soft spot for honey.

The Bible claims to be able to speak directly to our needs, and that's an experience which is heart-warming, nerve-tingling and sweet-tasting, all in one.'

Application and response

'If you have never read the Bible, why not give it a go? If you don't agree with it, fair enough, but at least you'll be able to decide for yourself what you really think about it.

Get a modern translation that is easy to understand, but don't start reading from the beginning! The Bible story centres on the person called Jesus and his life is written about in four short Bible books near the end; they are named after their authors – Matthew, Mark, Luke and John. Read about Jesus first and then the rest of it will make more sense.

Spiritual milk, meat and honey – try it!'

100 MILLION MESSAGES EVERY SECOND

Introduction

Aim:
To show that it isn't silly to pray, because God can listen to countless people talking to him at the same time. (*Note*: This could be part of a series on prayer – it would certainly be good to follow this with an assembly on how God answers prayer, perhaps by interviewing a colleague/church member on his or her personal experience of answered prayer.)

Preparation:
You will need a candle and matches; two or three 'sound-makers', eg bell, whistle; something colourful to display.

Content

Make a 'surprise' opening: say, sombrely, 'Let us pray. . .' Wait for everyone to close their eyes, then say, 'Hold on a minute! What if we all started praying different things at the same time? How could God listen to each one of us, not to mention the millions of other people round the world who are praying just at this moment? We probably don't imagine God with thousands of ears sticking out of his head, but how does he do it?'

Ask the pupils to close their eyes – not to pray this time, but to think about their left foot. What can they feel? Ask them to wriggle their toes. There are an average of 450 touch cells in every square inch of skin and, in addition, cells to measure temperature and pain. Most of the time we're not aware of them – unless we deliberately think about that part of our body or it starts to get uncomfortable or painful.

Light a candle and ask the group to look at it. Each eye has 120 million rod cells that respond to broad spectrum light. If it was pitch dark we could see a candle from several miles away. Display something colourful. There are a further seven million cone cells in our eyes that respond to colour.

Make some different noises . . . our ears have 25,000 sound receptor cells that are constantly sending messages to the brain about the sounds around us. All through the day they will be relaying teachers' or parents' voices to the brain – even if the brain doesn't particularly want to listen!

'Cells sensitive to touch, light, sound and lots more, are all constantly sending messages to your brain. In fact, your brain receives and processes 100 million messages a second! That's like listening to twice the population of Britain all talking at once! And only one tenth of one percent (one thousandth) of your brain is occupied with receiving those messages.'

Application and response

'One-thousandth of your brain handles 100 million messages a second. That's true whether you are a university professor or a road sweeper. If your brain can do that, don't you think that God, the creator of the universe, can handle a few million people talking to him at once?'

Prayer (see note on page 6): 'Dear God, thank you for being able and prepared to listen to each of us. Give us the confidence to know that you do hear us and will answer us. Amen.'

THE SLIME DIP

Introduction

Aim:
To help pupils understand what Christians believe about Jesus.

Preparation:
You will need to make up a 'slime dip' in a large glass or clear plastic jar, big enough to get your hand into. Fill it partly with washing-up liquid, then add sugar, flour, sauce, coconut, coffee, tea bags and generally any old thing you can find in your cupboard. The more disgusting your dip the more effective the visual aid.

By using a jar with a lid the dip can be used several times. However, remember that sugar can stick the lid to the top of the jar so free it with hot water beforehand to avoid embarrassment when you try to open it!

You will also need to bring a towel and wipes to clean up afterwards, and will need one ten-penny and two five-penny pieces.

Content

Say how generous you are feeling this morning. You have had a lovely breakfast and are generally feeling on top of the world. Because you are so happy you want to give somebody twenty pence to buy a Mars Bar. Ask for two volunteers (see note 8 on page 17). When they come to the front explain that there is one small catch and produce the slime dip.

Making sure the dip is clearly visible, drop the coins into the jar and ask one of the volunteers to get them out by hand. (Most will do it but don't push unnecessarily.) If the first one baulks at it, the second one may have a go. If there are no problems with the first one, make a lot of the second one acting as witness to how horribly slimy the dip really is.

Provide wipes and towels straight away for the volunteer to clean his or her hands. Wipe the coins and hand them over. Thank the volunteers and ask them to sit down.

Explain that the basic ingredient of the dip is something they all know and might even use each day – it's pure, clean and gentle washing-up liquid. Explain that it got all messed up when you added the HP sauce, coffee, tea bags etc but, fortunately, the volunteer was brave enough to reach down into the slimy mess and rescue the 20p in coins.

Application and response

'Christians believe that God created the world and that he made it a really good place to be. But it got all messed up by things like greed, envy, hatred and jealousy. And people, whom God thought were much more valuable than 10p or 5p coins, got all caught up in the mess. So he did something about it. The Bible says that God

→

58

became a man, Jesus, and came down into the messed-up world to rescue the messed-up people in it, and to clean them up.'

Go on to say what this has meant in your own experience, then conclude with something like the following:

'The Bible says we need never feel too messed up to be of value to God. Christians believe that Jesus is cleaning them up and sorting them out, and that he →

wants to do the same for anyone who asks him to.

I'm going to say a prayer now. Listen quietly to the words and, if you agree with them, make them your own. (See note on page 6.)

Dear God, thank you that you always accept us, even if we're not popular or seem to be failures. Help us when we fail. Please give us the strength to overcome the things we do that we know are wrong. Thank you for your help. Amen.'

THE MYSTERY OF THE 'MARY CELESTE'

Introduction

Aim:

To show that Christians believe God can be trusted even when bad things are happening to us.

Content

Retell this story in your own words.

One of the most famous sea mysteries of all time was that of the *Mary Celeste*. In November 1892 two ships set sail from New York. One was the *Mary Celeste* bound for Genoa in Italy. The captain was called Briggs and on this particular voyage he was accompanied by his wife and young daughter. One week after the departure of the *Mary Celeste* the other ship, the *Dei Gratia*, sailed for Gibraltar captained by Brigg's friend, Moorhouse.

One month later, Moorhouse sighted his friend's ship, the *Mary Celeste*, in the Atlantic off the Azores about 950 kilometres from Gibraltar. Her sails were raised but her movement in the breeze was so erratic that Moorhouse knew something was wrong.

A boarding party was sent on board the *Mary Celeste*. They found the ship completely deserted – only the lifeboat was missing. The ship was found to be seaworthy; there was enough food in the ship's store to have lasted for six months and there was plenty of fresh water. The ship's cargo was intact. They also found on board the boots, coats and oilskins of the crew. It looked as if the whole crew had left in a great hurry.

Why was the *Mary Celeste* abandoned? Why was no trace of the crew or the lifeboat ever found? Nobody knows, although many different and imaginative explanations have been put forward. The *Mary Celeste* still remains one of the great unsolved mysteries of the sea.

Application and response

'In life, things sometimes happen to us that are sad and puzzling and we wonder why. It's a mystery to us at the time. Some people might even say, "Why did God allow that to happen?" '

Illustrate this point by sharing from your own experience. Go on to share that a Christian is *not* someone who claims to have all the answers to everything, but does know that God can be trusted to help him or her even through the difficult times.

OUR FATHER! ?

Introduction

Aim:
To look at some common views of God and to introduce the Christian's view of God as 'Father'.

Preparation:
As you prepare for this assembly, bear in mind that some of the pupils may have had only bad experiences of what a father is like. Do not assume, therefore, that 'everyone knows what it's like to have a good father,' and avoid belittling or personalising other views that people may have of God.

You will need to transfer the four illustrations onto OHP acetates. This may be done either by tracing them or by using a photocopier to transfer the picture onto a special copier acetate. The acetates will look even better if you colour them with permanent ink OHP pens.

As part of your preparation you will also need to 'flesh out' the bare bones of the given input relating to each picture. Don't rely on being able to ad-lib it on the day.

Content

1 Talk about going to a local swimming pool and mention all the things you're not allowed to do there (eg running on edge, splashing others, pushing people in, kissing etc). 'All the really fun things are outlawed! And of course the life guards are there to blow their whistle at you the minute you overstep the mark. Most people ignore the life guard until either the whistle is blown or until they're drowning!

You quickly begin to take notice of the life guard when you're in difficulties.

A lot of people treat God like that (display God as divine rescuer) – ignore him most of the time but when difficulties come along – problems at home, difficult exams, being in danger—we quickly rattle off a prayer. There's nothing wrong with that; the problem is that as soon as we're out of difficulty we forget all about God again. But God is a lot more than a divine rescuer.

2 So maybe you've been swimming and now you're on your way home. You do something that you know you shouldn't – perhaps you kicked a dog, stole some sweets or went half-fare instead of full on the bus. Just as you leave the scene of the crime you see a policeman coming towards you. You think, "O good, someone to own up to!" Of course you don't! You think, "just keep walking, act natural and he'll never suspect me." I've met people who think of God only in terms of what they've done wrong (display God as a moral policeman). They believe that God exists, but think he's really only there to catch us out when we do wrong. But that gives a very one-sided view of God.'

3 Talk about a child (talk from personal experience if possible) who receives regular visits from a relative (grandmother?). 'When Gran appears she always brings sweets. Eventually the only reason that the child wants Gran to come is because she wants the sweets. And what happens? You've guessed it – all the child's teeth begin to rot so Gran stops bringing sweets which upsets the child who gets to resent Gran's "meanness". Many people see God like the child saw Gran (display God as Santa Claus). His only job is to bring good things into our lives (happiness, security, money, jobs etc) and when those things don't appear we get cross with him – even if the things that we want are in the end bad for us. But God is a lot more than Santa Claus.

4 A lot of people think of God as being an old man in the sky (acetate). He's up there . . . somewhere. But he's not very much in touch with what's going on and he's certainly got no interest in the lives of ordinary teenagers in the 1990s. All the evidence seems to suggest that he's a has-been; the buildings he lives in are old and falling down; the people who worship him all seem to be over sixty and the language that he understands is full of "thees", "thous" and "thines". Well, God *has* been around for a *very* long time, but he's much more than an old man in the sky.'

Application and response

'So what *is* God like? Well Jesus gave us a big clue in a prayer that he taught to his friends. He said that when we talk to God we should not call him "Life Guard", "Santa", "PC" or "Grandad" but our *Father*. That's what God wants to be to you – a good father: a good father who knows all about you, cares deeply about every aspect of your life and wants the best for you.'

If you feel it is appropriate (see note on page 6) ask people to listen to this prayer as you say it, and to make it their own if they want to.

Prayer: 'Almighty Father, thank you that you want to be a good Father to us. Help us to learn and understand more about your love for us. Amen.'

God as
divine rescuer

God as a moral policeman

God as
Santa Claus

God as an old man in the sky

7X: THE SECRET INGREDIENT

Introduction

Aim:
To stimulate thought about what Christians believe to be the most important 'ingredient' in life.

Preparation:
You will need to buy in advance three or four different brands of Cola (Coca Cola, Pepsi, a local supermarket brand, etc). On the day, you will need to have these poured out into separate tumblers, lined up on a table.

Content

Have the three or four tumblers of different brands of cola lined up on the table. Invite two volunteers (see note 8 on page 17) to a 'cola challenge'. Ask them to taste the drinks and decide which is the true Coca Cola. No matter whether they are successful or not, encourage applause for their efforts and ask them to go back to their seats.

Then go on to tell the story of 7X – the secret ingredient:

A few years ago the manufacturers of one of the most popular drinks in the world were celebrating the centenary of their product. Coca Cola is a favourite drink all over the world and if you have tasted Coca Cola then you have also tasted the secret ingredient 7X! In 1886 Dr John Pemberton produced the syrup essence for Coca Cola and had it sold as a soda fountain drink at Jacobs Pharmacy in Atlanta for five cents a glass. Not long after he sold his recipe for $50.

Today that same formula, helped by skilful advertising, has made billions of pounds from the bottles and cans of Coca Cola which are sold every day from Miami to Moscow, Toronto to Timbuktu.

On each can the manufacturers show the ingredients in their product and many other manufacturers have tried to copy it but none has ever produced anything which is exactly the same for there is one ingredient in Coca Cola which is a closely-guarded secret, the secret ingredient 7X.

As long as this remains a secret then, although others can make something which looks and tastes similar, the one thing they cannot make is Coca Cola.

Application and response

'Christians believe that there is a secret ingredient to life, something that will make life different and special for those who possess it. Jesus told his followers about it. He didn't sell the formula though, but freely told people about it. He didn't ask them to keep it a closely guarded secret, but encouraged them to tell their friends about it.

What is this secret ingredient? In a short time of quiet now, see if you can think what it could be!'

(Note: avoid spelling out the fact that Jesus himself is the 'special ingredient' to life, whose presence changes us completely. Hopefully, the air of mystery will lead to discussion among the pupils during the rest of the day.)

Christmas . . .

A GIFT AT CHRISTMAS

Introduction

Aim:
To show why Christians celebrate Christmas.

Preparation:
You will need some props for this assembly: three party hats, three Mars Bars for prizes, three cups and a jug of water.

You will also need the help of three pupils. Either arrange this with them in advance or, if you know the school well enough and are confident to do so, select three volunteers on the day (see point 8 on page 17).

Content

Explain that Christmas is a time for fun and parties and that today's assembly will be no exception. Select three volunteers from the audience. As you introduce the game put the hats on the volunteers and explain that the audience will act as judges for the game. The volunteers have to gargle the first line of the carol, 'Silent Night' and the best will receive a prize. (You may need to sing the beginning of the carol yourself, to remind them of the tune – and to break the 'silence' barrier.)

Do the competition and find the winner, but give *all* the volunteers a prize.

Application and response

'Christmas is about fun, and about giving and receiving presents. At Christmas, Christians celebrate the greatest gift they believe was ever given – a person, Jesus. Christians believe he came to show us how much God loves us and to put us back in touch with God. Jesus is a gift God wants to give to everybody, no matter whether or not we "deserve" it, just as everyone got a prize in the game just now. That's why it's such a happy festival for Christians.

We'll spend a few moments in quiet now. Think about the presents you'll be giving this Christmas and the happiness they will bring to people. Or think about God's present to us of Jesus, and of how you think God hopes we might respond. If you would like to, talk to him about it in your mind.'

MARY'S VISITOR

Introduction

Aim:

This was written to try to show that without Mary's trust in God and her willingness to go through with a rather mind-boggling, embarrassing, and humanly incredible plan, we would have no Christ and therefore no Christmas to celebrate. It also highlights the fact that Christmas wasn't the 'sanitised sweet story' of today's commercialism, but in the eyes of Mary's neighbours – and even, initially, in Joseph's eyes – a scandal!

Preparation:

You will need the following props: Housecoat, headscarf, broom, duster, radio, chair, small table, wine/gin bottle, glasses, Yellow Pages, angel outfit with big 'G' emblazoned on the front.

And the following actors: Narrator (N), Mary (M), Angel Gabriel (G), Bible reader (B).

Content

N: (*read like a Radio One DJ*) It's Friday afternoon in downtown Nazareth. At Number 16 Camel Terrace, Mary is busy doing the housework while listening to her favourite Hebrew melodies on Radio Rabbi . . . the Number One Sound! Little does she know that someone special is winging his way to bring her some rather startling news. . . (*Exit N and enter M*).

(*Mary, dressed in housecoat, headscarf, broom in one hand, duster in the other, is cleaning the house with pop music blaring from radio*)

M: Cor, just look at the muck in 'ere . . . that Joseph! Wish he'd leave them blinkin' goats outside!

(*G appears at door dressed in white robe, sandals, halo etc . . . clutching Yellow Pages.*)

G: (*softly spoken*) Hail Mary!

(*Mary doesn't hear*)

G: (*steps into room and says a bit louder*) Hail Mary!

(*M looks up but doesn't see G*)

M: That you, Joseph? (*no reply so shrugs shoulders and continues cleaning*)

G: (*half shouts*) Hail Mary!

M: (*looks out of window, shakes head with puzzled look and says*) What hail? Don't be so silly Joseph, it's perfectly sunny outside!

G: (*jumps in front of Mary who screams and drops duster and broom*) HAIL MARY!! (*shouted really loud*)

M: Aaah! Who are you? What are you doin' 'ere? Gave me a dreadful fright. . . (*continues to mutter with hand on heart*)

G: (*turns off radio and says in refined voice*) Hail, most highly favoured, the Lord is with thee. . .

(*M looks confused and turns round expecting to see God!*)

M: (*looking frightened*) Yer what?

G: Don't be afraid Mary . . . you have found favour with God. . . (*seeing that this is going to be hard work G pushes M into nearby chair and*

pours them both a drink) . . . Here I think you' better sit down. . .
(*Mary gulps the drink and wonders what on earth G is going to say*)

G: You are going to be with child and . . .

M: (*screams and jumps up*) Now just watch it . . . who's been saying things?
(*G pushes her back into the chair*)

G: Calm down, old girl. The child will be the son of the most High God and he will be given the throne of his father David (*grandly stated*)

M: David? David? My bloke's name is Joseph!

G: (*ignoring her*) He will reign over the house of Jacob forever and ever and his kingdom will have no end.

M: (*more interested*) Mmmm . . .palaces . . . thrones. . . ? . . . And how will this king . . . this baby arrive? . . . I'm . . . um . . . I mean . . . we ain't married yet (*slightly embarrassed*)

G: (*moves closer to Mary and says dramatically*) The Holy Spirit shall come upon you and the power of the Most High will overshadow you. . .
(*G leans over M who slithers down in chair looking very worried*) . . . so the Holy One born to you will be God's Son and you will name him . . . (*G pauses and then says with grandeur*) . . . Jesus!

M: (*cackles loudly and slaps G on the back*) Don't be so daft! With a name like that, he won't half get ribbed at school!
(*M pushes G out of the way, picks up broom and duster and recommences cleaning*)

M: Now a joke's a joke, mate, but really I've got loads to do so if you don't mind, 'op it like a little angel . . .
(*realises pun and cackles*) . . . like an angel, eh! ! . . . get it? . . . An angel. . . What a pun! !
(*G not amused and, looking fed up, opens Yellow Pages*)

G: But . . . I'm sure I've got the right address . . . V . . . V . . . Virgin Atlantic . . . Virgin Records. . . Virgin Marys . . . Ah! . . . mmmm . . . Oh!
(*G exits scratching his head with bemused expression*)

M: (*still muttering and laughing to herself*) Gonna have a baby! . . . What a joker! . . . Jesus too! . . . What a name! . . . Well, I never! ! . . .
(*Exit M*)
(*Enter B and N*)

Application and response

N: What a good job the real Mary wasn't so busy, so suspicious of Gabriel, and so unsure of God, otherwise we might never have had a Christmas. Let's hear what really happened. . .

B: (reads Luke 1:26–38.)

POODLES AND MUSHROOMS

Introduction

Aim:
To explore the real meaning of Christmas.

Preparation:
You will need:
- the filmstrip, *X-ray Eyes*, produced by Scripture Union. You should be able to hire it from any Christian book shop. In case of difficulty contact Scripture Union Mail Order, 9–11 Clothier Road, Brislington, Bristol, BS4 5RL.
- a projector and cassette player capable of producing sufficient good quality volume to fill the assembly hall (see section on using audio-visual aids, pages 21–23).
- a pre-selected assortment of Christmas cards.
- a 'guest' whom you bring with you – someone who has become a Christian since last year and is prepared to say what new meaning Christmas will have for him or her this year.

Note: There is probably more material in this outline than you will be able to use in one assembly. Select in advance the sections you will use, and prepare accordingly.

Content

'Christmas can be a real hassle. It lasts so long; from the crackers appearing in the shops on 1st September through to the decorations coming down in mid-January. Why do we bother? What's it all about?

A survey was done recently of the types of pictures that appear on Christmas cards. (Hold up a handful.) The results were that out of an average bunch of fifty cards, forty-six are of various scenes including things like snow, holly, robins, horses, coaches and horses, Father Christmas, small children, dolls, poodles with holly, and even reindeer in a field of mushrooms!

Four were 'religious'. In the survey, a typical selection would be: one of carol singers, one of a child angel wearing eyeshadow, one of a baby in a cradle surrounded by children and two lambs, and one of three wise men.

If you had only that lot to go on, what would you think Christmas was all about?'

Show the filmstrip, *Babies* (four minutes), from *X-ray Eyes*.

Application and response

Pick up the Christmas card theme again, showing one that accurately reflects the meaning of Christmas. Introduce your guest as 'a friend who has become a Christian since last Christmas'. Ask him or her to say briefly how Christmas will be different for them this year.

CHRISTMAS IS COMING!

Introduction

Aim:

To encourage pupils to decide what meaning they will give to Christmas.

Preparation:

The poems in this assembly are more effective if read by a second person or by three Christian pupils you know in the school. Take time to contact suitable people and to arrange the assembly with them.

Content

Introduce the assembly with a few light thoughts on the approaching Christmas celebration and its increasing commercialism.

Then go on to present the next two items, with a short commentary in between along the lines of that scripted.

COLOSSAL CONSUMER CHRISTMAS

It's a colossal
Consumer Christmas,
All spending records broken.
But on Christmas morning,
It's the shops that should smile
Every time
The word thank-you is spoken.

How much is a jumper in Wool Worth?
Does your Mother really care?
If we developed a new superdrug,
Would the two-thirds world
Get their share?

We'll give you full marks for your Spend, Sir,

It's your Gateway to the top.
You hope that your Visa will give Access,
But is plastic the Safeway to shop?

It's a colossal
Consumer Christmas
All spending records broken,
But on Christmas morning
It's the shops that should smile
Every time
The word thank-you is spoken.

It's the big spender's natural Habitat,
So where will your Body Shop next?
You can be sure that the shareholders' pensions
Will be Retail-Price-Indexed.

They're going insane down at Sainsbury's,
At Bejam they've jammed every till.
You won't be laughing
All the way to the bank:
But you can bet your Boots that they will!

'But I believe Christmas is not just about money and buying presents – it's about God. At least that's what I was told! Christmas has *something* to do with God.'

Read the poem 'God is Dog spelt backwards.'

GOD IS DOG SPELT BACKWARDS

We were so glad to welcome him
On Christmas day.
It was like having a new member
Of the family.
He looked so tiny and helpless:
It made you just want to pick him up
And cuddle him.

We made promises, of course;
Said we'd make room for him in our
    home,
Said we'd alter our routines
To fit him in,
Said we'd take a walk with him
Each day.

But the novelty soon began
To wear off.
By New Year, we were mentioning him
Less often,
Daily chores were less of a thrill
More of a reluctant duty.
By February he was unwanted
By March we had abandoned him
    completely.

We should have read the warnings
We should have counted the cost
A God is for life
Not just for Christmas.

Application and response

'So who decides what Christmas is all about? Who chooses whether it's a five-day booze up, a credit card spending spree, a once-a-year visit to church, a family holiday? Who chooses? You do!

Christmas is what you make of it. It's not something that's thrown at you whether you like it or not. It isn't something that comes ready-packaged, unchangeable and fixed. We choose what's important and what it can mean for ourselves. It's up to you. Christmas is what *you* make it.' Read the poem *Behold I Stand*.   →

BEHOLD I STAND

When the night is deep
With the sense of Christmas
And expectancy hangs heavy
On every breath
Behold I stand at the door and knock.

When the floor is knee deep
In discarded wrapping paper
And the new books are open at page
    one
And the new toys are already broken
Behold I stand at the door and knock.

When the family is squashed
Elbow to elbow
Around the table
And the furious rush for food is over
And the only word that can describe the
    feeling
Is full
Behold I stand at the door and knock.

And when Christmas is over
And the television is silent
For the first time in two days
And who sent which card to whom
Is forgotten until next year
Behold I stand at the door

And when the nation has finished
    celebrating
Christmas without Christ
A birthday
Without a birth
The coming of a Kingdom
Without a King
And when I am
Forgotten
Despised
Rejected
Crucified

Behold I stand.

Easter...

TRUTH – STRANGER THAN FICTION!

Introduction

Aim:
To challenge pupils to think about the possibility of the resurrection of Jesus.

Content

Introduce the assembly by asking, 'Have you ever been told to do something you thought was really stupid, only to find it was actually very sensible? "Brush your teeth." "Take an umbrella." "Phone up if you miss the nine o'clock train."

Sometimes we come across other people who seem cranks and fanatics – they've got some weird idea and they try to convince everyone else that it's true. Well, let me tell you about a few people who others thought were cranks but whose ideas turned out to be right.

- When Christopher Columbus sailed off to find America everyone thought he was crazy. At that time, people thought the world was flat and that, after sailing across the Atlantic Ocean, Columbus would just drop off the edge and disappear for ever! But Columbus was proved right.
- Leonardo da Vinci was a famous painter and artist but he also drew plans for the most incredible machines. Everyone at the time thought he was stupid. They saw his drawings of a parachute, a helicopter and a submarine and thought, 'Impossible; no one could ever make something that would do that.' But da Vinci was proved right.
- People said to Orville and Wilbur Wright, the two brothers who built the first American aeroplane, that if humans were meant to fly they'd have wings. People said that their aeroplane would never get off the ground, that flight by machines heavier than air was utterly impossible. But the Wright brothers were proved right.
- Fifteen years ago, if someone had said that by using hairspray or deodorant you'd be helping to destroy part of the earth's atmosphere, no one would have believed it. But it's true! Because people didn't understand, they thought it was foolish to say such things but now most people use 'ozone friendly' aerosols.

Application and response

'When Jesus said he'd rise from the dead after three days, people just didn't think it was possible and they laughed at him. When he was crucified they thought that was the end of him. Jesus was dead and buried. But Christians believe that he came to life again.

Could that really have happened? Are we prepared to check out the facts?'

WOULD YOU BELIEVE IT?

Introduction

Aim:
To encourage pupils not to dismiss the claim of Christians that Jesus rose from the dead, even though it seems, at first sight, unlikely.

Preparation:
You will need to prepare six cards (A3 size) with a large letter 'T' on each and six cards with a large letter 'F'. You will need six volunteers at the front with you (see point 8 on page 17).

Content

Give each of these one 'T' (True) card and one 'F' (False) card. Explain that you are going to read a number of short stories or statements and they must decide whether each is true (in which case they raise the 'T' card) or false (in which case they raise the 'F' card).

The stories/statements:

The average human being produces up to one pint of saliva every day.

(FALSE: two to three pints)

The firemen's strike of 1978 made possible one of the great animal rescue attempts of all time. Valiantly, the British Army had taken over emergency firefighting and on 14 January they were called out by an elderly lady in South London to retrieve her cat which had become trapped up a tree. They arrived with impressive haste and soon discharged their duty. So grateful was the lady that she invited them all in for tea. Driving off later, with fond farewells completed, they ran over the cat and killed it.

(TRUE)

While teething, toddler Graham Kenton of Hayes, Middlesex developed an unfortunate liking for chewing paper clips. The inevitable happened and on 3 July 1981 he swallowed a clip, and was promptly rushed to hospital for an X-Ray. Imagine his mother's surprise when the contents of his stomach were found to contain three paper clips, a marble, the top of a biro and an old back door key!

(FALSE)

In 1978 workers were sent to dredge a murky stretch of the Chesterfield-Stockwith canal. Their task was to remove all the rubbish and leave the canal clear. They were soon disturbed during their tea break by a policeman who said he was investigating a giant whirlpool in the canal. When they got back, however, the whirlpool had gone and so had a one-and-a-half mile stretch of the canal. In its place was a vast expanse of mud thickly punctuated with old prams, bedsteads and rusting bicycle accessories. In addition to this the workmen found a flotilla of irate holidaymakers, stranded on their boats in a brown sludge.

They discovered that among the first pieces of junk they hauled out had been the 200-year-old plug that had ensured the canal's continuing existence. 'We didn't know there was a plug', said one workman explaining that all the records had been lost in a fire during the war. 'Anything can happen on a canal', a spokesman for the British Waterways Board said afterwards.

(TRUE)

Kung Fu expert Kori Osoko of Japan demolished an entire (condemned) five storey office building with his bare hands and feet. The demolition job was part of the 1979 Festival of Oriental Martial Arts and Kori Osoko took three days and five hours to complete the demolition.

(FALSE)

In 1978 Mr Christopher Fleming – burglar extraordinaire – went to work. His intention was to break into a Chinese restaurant at Tiverton in Devon via a kitchen window, remove as many notes as possible from the till and leave by the same route. In a manoeuvre that required breathtaking agility, he climbed through the window, lost his balance and fell into a chip fryer. Covered in grease, he clambered out and dripped his way to the till. Unable to find any notes, he loaded up with £20 in bulky loose change and, with the grease now congealing, walked out of the restaurant straight into the arms of a policeman.

(TRUE)

In 1985 Martin Wilmot – a native of New York – landed at Heathrow Airport to visit his sister, Louise, who had settled in Cornwall. Mr Wilmot hired a car at the airport to complete his journey to Penzance, where his sister was awaiting him. Unfortunately, Mr Wilmot had never driven a car which did not have an automatic gearbox and was therefore unused to having to change gear. Consequently he completed the entire journey in second gear at a top speed of twenty-five miles per hour, causing approximately £3,000 worth of damage to the car's engine and transmission as well as making the journey last twelve hours instead of the expected five-and-a-half!

(FALSE – but based on a true story)

Application and response

'It is easy to dismiss the seemingly impossible but sometimes, when you do, you dismiss the truth!

Loads of people just dismiss the resurrection of Jesus as untrue because it seems unlikely.

A few years ago a lawyer called Frank Morrison decided to use his legal skills to build a case proving that Jesus could not possibly have come alive again after such a public death. After a long time researching, this is what he said:

"The opportunity came to study the life of Christ as I had long wanted to study it . . . to sift some of the evidence at first hand, and to form my own judgement. . . I will only say that it effected a revolution in my thought. Things emerged from that old-world story which previously I should have thought impossible. Slowly but very definitely the conviction grew that the drama of those unforgettable weeks of human history was stranger and deeper than it seemed."

The evidence that lawyer found suggested that Jesus did defeat death and is still alive today. Why not examine the evidence for yourself?'

THE COST OF LOVE

Introduction

Aim:
To explain what Good Friday means to Christians.

Preparation:
You will need a copy of the story printed below, so that you can read it out.

You will also need to photocopy the picture of Christ onto an acetate sheet.

Check that you will be able to use an overhead projector and that the screen and projector will be set up ready for you (or arrange to go in early enough to set it up yourself). Take a spare projector bulb with you, in case of disasters!

Content

Introduce the following story with a very brief introduction: 'Good Friday speaks to Christians of a very powerful love – love so powerful that it led to self-sacrifice.'

Then read this story, taken from *Miracle on the River Kwai*, by Ernest Gordon. Set the scene: It is a true story about some British soldiers who were captured by the Japanese in the Second World War. They are outside the prisoner of war camp.

'The day's work had ended; the tools were being counted, as usual. As the party was about to be dismissed, the Japanese guard shouted that a shovel was missing. He insisted that someone had stolen it to sell to the Thais. Striding up and down before the men, he ranted and denounced them for their wickedness and, most unforgivable of all, their ingratitude to the Emperor. As he raved, he worked himself up into a paranoid fury. Screaming in broken English, he demanded that the guilty one step forward to take his punishment. No one moved; the guard's rage reached new heights of violence.

"All die! All die!" he shrieked.

To show that he meant what he said, he cocked his rifle, put it to his shoulder and looked down the sights ready to fire at the first man at the end of the line.

At that moment a soldier stepped forward, stood stiffly to attention and said calmly, "I did it." The guard unleashed all his whipped-up hate; he kicked the helpless prisoner and beat him with his fists. Still the soldier stood rigidly to attention, with the blood streaming down his face. His silence goaded the guard to an excess of rage. Seizing his rifle by the barrel, he lifted it high over his head and, with a final blow, brought it down on the skull of the soldier, who sank limply to the ground and did not move. Although it was perfectly clear that he was dead, the guard continued to beat him and stopped only when exhausted.

The men of the work detail picked up their comrade's body, shouldered their tools and marched back to camp. When the tools were counted again at the guard house no shovel was missing.'

Application and response

Pause, then go on to read Isaiah 53:4–9, 12. (The Good News version is the best one to use because it is more easily understood on its first hearing. It is printed below.) As you read the passage, place the acetate of Jesus on the cross onto the OHP:

'He endured the suffering that should
    have been ours,
  the pain that we should have borne.
All the while we thought that his suffering
    was punishment sent by God.
But because of our sins he was
    wounded,
  beaten because of the evil we did.
We are healed by the punishment he
    suffered,
  made whole by the blows he received.
All of us were like sheep that were lost,
  each of us going his own way.
But the Lord made the punishment fall
    on him,
  the punishment all of us deserved.
He was treated harshly, but endured it
    humbly;
  he never said a word.
Like a lamb about to be slaughtered,
like a sheep about to be sheared,
  he never said a word.
He was arrested and sentenced and led
    off to die,
  and no one cared about his fate.
He was put to death for the sins of our
    people.
He was placed in a grave with evil men,
  he was buried with the rich,
even though he had never committed a
    crime
  or ever told a lie.'

He willingly gave his life
  and shared the fate of evil men.
He took the place of many sinners
  and prayed that they might be
    forgiven.'

There is no need to say any more; simply conclude with the statement: 'Real love costs everything.'

Part Three

ADDITIONAL RESOURCE MATERIAL

WHAT'S THE POINT?

This dramatic reading must proceed at a reasonable pace – be careful not to let it drag. Speed up as you read through section 5 and increase volume until you shout, 'What's the point of it all?'

Throughout the reading a metronome could be ticking away on stage like a clock.

1 Get up
   Get washed
   Get dressed
   Breakfast
   Bus
   School
   Assembly
   Maths
   Geography
   Lunch
   Rice pudding and prunes
   RE
   Chemistry
   Home
   Tea
   TV
   Homework
   TV
   Bed

   (PAUSE)

2 Get up
   Get washed
   Get dressed
   Breakfast
   Bus
   School
   Physics
   PE
   Lunch

Fight
English
French
Detention
Home
TV
Tea
TV
Phone Girlfriend/Boyfriend
TV
Homework
Bed

(PAUSE)

3 Weekend
   Get up
   Lunch
   Party
   Drink
   Food
   Dance
   Food
   Drink
   Ill
   Sick
   Bed

   (PAUSE)

4 Wake up
   Hangover
   Coffee
   Bed

   (PAUSE)

5 Get up
   Get washed

Get dressed
Breakfast
Bus
School
6 years?
College?
University?
Job?
Dole Queue

Girlfriend/Boyfriend
Serious
Married
Kids
Mortgage
Bills
No Money
Bored! 65 . . . (shout) WHAT'S
   THE POINT OF IT ALL ? ? ?

THE SAUSAGE SKETCH

This sketch works best without introduction. Actors enter from opposite ends of the hall. (Check that the school is happy with this arrangement.) It has only two characters (can be either male or female) – timeless 'market stall' characters. A hand-held placard (and daft hats) are enough props.

Asking a volunteer to eat the small sausage at the end is also fun. Take the big one home and freeze it till the next time!

CAST: Sandwich Board Man 1
        (Eat at Joe's)
        Sandwich Board Man 2
        (Eat at Fred's)

Enter Man 1. He takes up a position of maximum visibility and begins to call, in his best 'market place' manner.

Man 1:   Roll up, roll up! Where do you find the juiciest, fattest sausages in the world? Eat at Joe's!

Fried eggy bread to tingle your taste buds. Eat at Joe's! Where mugs are mugs and not egg cups, and the tea is thick and strong. Eat at Joe's!

Man 2:   Roll up, roll up. Where do you find the juiciest, fattest sausages in the world? Eat at Fred's! Fried eggy. . .

Man 1:   Excuse me, excuse me, please!

Man 2:   What do you want, little man?

Man 1:   I got here first, you know.

Man 2:   So?

Man 1, being considerably shorter than Man 2, fetches a folding stool and stands on it to talk to his rival. Optional, depending on your actors.

Man 1:   So, I got here first, didn't I? And besides. . .

Man 2:   Yeah?

Man 1:	Everyone knows that Joe's beats all his foes.
Man 2:	Take it as read, that Fred knocks Joe's on the head.
Man 1:	That, Sir, is a matter of opinion.
Man 2:	That, Sir, is a matter of fact.
Man 1:	Listen mate, I just happen to have in my pocket here, a prime example of Joe's expertise.

He produces a freshly-cooked chipolata.

| Man 1: | Beat that! |

Man 2 produces a large curved pork sausage from around his neck and gloats.

Man 1:	Mine tastes better. That's what counts.
Man 2:	That, Sir, is a matter of opinion.
Man 1:	That, Sir, is a matter of Fact.
Man 2:	Opinion!
Man 1:	Fact!
Man 2:	Opinion!
Man 1:	Fact!

MADE FOR. . .

Two people are needed for this sketch, one to speak and one to mime. As one speaks the other reaches into a bag, pulls out the item and performs the appropriate actions.

ITEM

Clock	Made (*Pause while clock is produced*) to keep time
Teddy	Made to cuddle
Phone	Made to keep in touch
Tissue	Made for (*sneeze till hole in middle*)
Deodorant	Made to kill the smell (*sniff armpit*)
Jacket	Made to measure ? ? (*too small*)
Twix	Made for the dentist (*wince*)
Helmet	Made for protection
Torch	Made for the dark
£10 note	Made to go (*1 snatches 2*)
Clockwork toy	Made to entertain
Cassette music	Made to boogie to (1 *turns off*)
Wine	Made to pickle the liver!
Cigarette	Made to shorten your life by 5 minutes each.
People	Made (*Pause, drop to knees and bow head*) to know God.

A MODERN PARABLE OF THE GOOD SAMARITAN

This monologue can easily be
adapted for other teams, inserting
new names, players and club
colours into the text. It is
especially good where strong
rivalry exists between local clubs.

At a soccer match down at *Roker*
Noted for punch-ups and brawls
Mr and Mrs McKenzie
   (*Enter McKenzie family*)
Took young Scottie to watch the
 football.

Sunderland were playing
 Newcastle
And as the team came into view,
'Up with *Geordies!*' yelled Scottie,
'Get in – show 'em what you can do!'
   (*Jump up and down*)

The whistle blew – the game had
 begun,
The crowd shouted and roared.
Then, up the sidelines came (*name
of current striker*),
Kicked the ball . . . and, yes! he
 scored! (*Everyone cheers*)

The *Sunderland* fans weren't too
 happy
And soon the scuffles began,
'Down with the *Maccums!*' yelled
 Scottie (*Shakes fist*)
His father said, 'Shut up, young
 man.'

'You'll have them doing us over
If they hear you shouting like that.'
And just at that very moment
   (*Enter Sunderland*)

They were surrounded by *red* and
 white hats.

'Oh blimey!' cried Mr McKenzie
While his wife went into a faint,
'Which of you's insulting our team
 like?'
Scottie just smiled like a saint.
   (*Cheesy grin*)

The *Sunderland* fans grabbed
 young Scottie
And disappeared into the crowd
They gave him a bit of a dusting
And left him in a heap on the
 ground.

A *United* supporter walked past
 him (*Enter United supporter*)
But was too scared to help the poor
 lad.
The *red* and *white* hats made him
 dizzy
And his stomach felt really quite
 bad. (*Clutch stomach*)

His mum was still in hysterics
   (*Wife screams*)
And his father had gone for a beer.
   (*Father leaves*)
He said it would strengthen his
 nerve
But it was really out of cold fear.

Then up came an old *Sunderland*
 fan
Saw the boy all dirty and sore.
He felt right sorry for young Scottie
And picked him up off the floor.

He gave him a drink from his hip
  flask
And wiped the mud from his face.
'Where's your folks?' asked the old
  man,
'Can't leave you alone in this
  place.'

At long last came the grand reunion
                    (*Enter Mum and Dad*)
With Mother still blowing her nose
                    (*Mum blows nose*)

And Dad, on his third pint of
  Guinness
Just as the match came to a close.

'A three-all draw,' said the
  announcer
Amid the boos and the cheers,
                    (*Old man leaves*)
'Well, the *Maccums* aren't *all* bad'
  said Scottie
But the kind old man had
  disappeared.

A SENSE OF URGENCY

Late in 1940 three Motor Torpedo
Boats (MTBs) were making their
way to the Royal Navy Base at
Tobermory Bay. On Board MTB
559 was Lieutenant-Commander
Head and like all the other officers
and men he had never been in
action. As the Commander of this
force his job was going to be to train
them to meet anything they could
expect from the enemy. However,
at that particular time, his main
fear was what would happen when
they got to the base and met 'The
Terror of Tobermory' otherwise
known as Commodore Sir George
Stephenson, the base Commander
who was in overall charge of their
training. Sir George was a legend
in his own time. At the age now of
sixty-two he had won a reputation
for strict discipline and incredible
bravery. Earlier that year he had
spent forty-eight hours on the
Dunkirk beaches helping to rescue
the British Army trapped there.

Lieutenant-Commander Head
was determined to be ready for 'The
Terror' and brought his three ships
neatly to their mooring with his
own boat in the middle of the other
two. Orders were issued to have
everything absolutely spotless and
shipshape for the arrival of Sir
George. A rating with a mop was
placed near the bows of MTB 559
to clear up any last-minute mess.

When the cry came,
'Commander's barge approaching',
everyone braced themselves but
nothing happened. The barge
seemed to have disappeared.
Suddenly the rating at the bow
looked down and to his horror the
gold braided cap and bewhiskered
face of Sir George appeared over
the bow when everyone had
expected him to arrive the usual
way over the stern. 'The Terror'
exploded into action.

'I want the ship's mincer and this
ship is on fire . . . Move!'

As Sir George charged towards the bridge chaos broke out on MTB 559. Bewildered ratings rushed to the galley for the mincer and officers fell over each other in an attempt to rig hoses and prepare extinguishers to fight a non-existent fire. Sir George now fired his next shot.

'I don't believe it. This ship is still on fire and about to blow up. Do I have to operate these things myself?' The men all looked at him in disbelief. Surely he couldn't mean that they actually had to start up the fire hoses and let off the extinguishers on their spotless vessel? Indeed, that was what he wanted and MTB 559 now became covered with sea water and foam, immaculate uniforms were stained and the crews of the other two MTBs were enjoying the sight with great joy. Sir George, however, did not intend to let them enjoy the spectacle for long.

'You are in danger of being set on fire,' he yelled to them. 'Cut loose and I want your ships' boats overboard under sail.'

This meant separating from the MTBs in the middle. The problems of freeing from moorings, lowering the boats and making a makeshift sail from a bedsheet kept the sailors who had been spectators fully occupied as Sir George called for his barge and left the scene of confusion, anger and exhaustion.

Later that day, the officers met Sir George in his rooms. Lieutenant-Commander Head wryly admitted that Sir George had certainly put them into a panic. Sir George corrected him.

'Not panic, my dear boy, just a sense of urgency.'

SOCRATES AND THE TRAVELLERS

The philosopher Socrates was resting in the shade of a large olive tree one hot afternoon, when he was approached by a traveller making his way towards Athens.

'Tell me!' said the traveller, 'What sort of people live in Athens?'

Socrates looked up at him and replied, 'Where do you come from?'

'I come from Argos,' he answered.

'What are the people like in Argos?' asked Socrates.

'Awful!' he exlaimed. 'They're a lot of quarrelsome, unsociable, lying layabouts.'

Socrates pondered awhile as he studied the man, and then said, slowly, 'I'm sorry to tell you, but you'll find the people of Athens just the same.'

Presently another traveller came by and asked a similar question. Again, Socrates inquired where he came from.

'I come from Argos,' came the reply.

'What are the people like there?' asked Socrates.

'Charming!' answered the traveller. 'The people of Argos are kind, gentle, friendly, honest and hardworking.'

Socrates smiled and said, 'I'm pleased to tell you, my friend, that you'll find the people of Athens are much the same.'

ARE YOU SURE?

The following are statements found on insurance forms where car drivers attempted to summarise the details of an accident. Select four or five of these for inclusion in any one assembly.

Note: Before using these illustrations, check with a teacher that it will be all right to do so. If a pupil has just been involved in a car accident, or a member of his or her family has, you will need to rethink your illustrations.

- 'Coming home I drove into the wrong house and collided with a tree I don't have.'
- 'I thought my window was down, but I found it was up when I put my head through it.'
- 'I collided with a stationary truck coming the other way.'
- 'The guy was all over the road. I had to swerve a number of times before I hit him.'
- 'In an attempt to kill a fly, I drove into a telegraph pole.'
- 'I had been shopping for plants all day and was on my way home. As I reached the intersection a hedge sprang up, obscuring my vision and I did not see the other car.'
- 'I had been driving for forty years when I fell asleep at the wheel and had an accident.'
- 'My car was legally parked as it backed into the other vehicle.'
- 'An invisible car came out of nowhere, struck my car and vanished.'
- 'I told the police that I was not injured, but on removing my hat found I had a fractured skull.'
- 'The pedestrian had no idea which way to run, so I ran over him.'
- 'The indirect cause of the accident was a little guy in a small car with a big mouth.'
- 'I was thrown from my car as it left the road. I was later found in a ditch by some stray cows.'
- 'The other car collided with mine without giving warning of its intention.'

THE 'IMPOSSIBALL' ASSEMBLY

Ask for two 'athletic' pupils to volunteer to take part in a game of skill and endurance. When they come up, produce the 'Impossiball' (available at all good toyshops). Many of the pupils will know what it is, but carry on anyway and stress the fact that this looks like an ordinary ball and there is nothing which appears to be wrong with it. Place the pupils a few feet apart and ask them to play 'catch' by bouncing the ball midway between them. Appoint a 'scorekeeper'. The ball will bounce off course naturally (it has a biased weight inside). Carry on until one person reaches, say, five 'catches'. This provides a laugh as it will bounce all over the place, including offstage! !

POEMS

Gimme, gimme, gimme temptation!

Like a microwave oven,
It starts to cook
On the inside.
Like the small ads
In the tabloids
It offers
What it can't provide.
Like queues
On the M25,
It brings the best plans
To a halt.
Like a badly brought up
Tennis star,
It never admits
To a fault.
Like a book club
Joined in error,
It won't let you rest
Until you're dead.

Like a topless
Liquidiser,
Its effects
Are quickly wide-spread.
Like cut-price
Plastic surgery,
Its after
Is worse than before,
Like any well-managed
Pop star,
It always leaves you
Wanting more.

Like the shepherd's
Red sky at night
It promises delight
At sunrise.
But,
Like the sleeping dog
That it is,
It lies.